WHAT I DID LAST SUMMER

BY A.R. GURNEY

DRAMATISTS
PLAY SERVICE
INC.

WHAT I DID LAST SUMMER
Copyright © 1983, A.R. Gurney
Copyright © 1981, A.R. Gurney
as an unpublished dramatic composition

All Rights Reserved

CAUTION: Professionals and amateurs are hereby warned that performance of WHAT I DID LAST SUMMER is subject to payment of a royalty. It is fully protected under the copyright laws of the United States of America, and of all countries covered by the International Copyright Union (including the Dominion of Canada and the rest of the British Commonwealth), and of all countries covered by the Pan-American Copyright Convention, the Universal Copyright Convention, the Berne Convention, and of all countries with which the United States has reciprocal copyright relations. All rights, including professional/amateur stage rights, motion picture, recitation, lecturing, public reading, radio broadcasting, television, video or sound recording, all other forms of mechanical or electronic reproduction, such as CD-ROM, CD-I, DVD, information storage and retrieval systems and photocopying, and the rights of translation into foreign languages, are strictly reserved. Particular emphasis is placed upon the matter of readings, permission for which must be secured from the Author's agent in writing.

The English language stock and amateur stage performance rights in the United States, its territories, possessions and Canada for WHAT I DID LAST SUMMER are controlled exclusively by DRAMATISTS PLAY SERVICE, INC., 440 Park Avenue South, New York, NY 10016. No professional or nonprofessional performance of the Play may be given without obtaining in advance the written permission of DRAMATISTS PLAY SERVICE, INC., and paying the requisite fee.

Inquiries concerning all other rights should be addressed to William Morris Agency, Inc., 1325 Avenue of the Americas, 15th Floor, New York, NY 10019. Attn: Peter Franklin.

SPECIAL NOTE

Anyone receiving permission to produce WHAT I DID LAST SUMMER is required to give credit to the Author as sole and exclusive Author of the Play on the title page of all programs distributed in connection with performances of the Play and in all instances in which the title of the Play appears for purposes of advertising, publicizing or otherwise exploiting the Play and/or a production thereof. The name of the Author must appear on a separate line, in which no other name appears, immediately beneath the title and in size of type equal to 50% of the size of the largest, most prominent letter used for the title of the Play. No person, firm or entity may receive credit larger or more prominent than that accorded the Author.

SPECIAL NOTE ON SONGS AND RECORDINGS

For performances of copyrighted songs, arrangements or recordings mentioned in this Play, the permission of the copyright owner(s) must be obtained. Other songs, arrangements or recordings may be substituted provided permission from the copyright owner(s) of such songs, arrangements or recordings is obtained; or songs, arrangements or recordings in the public domain may be substituted.

WHAT I DID LAST SUMMER was first produced as a play-in-progress at the Circle Repertory Company in New York City in November, 1981, directed by Porter Van Zandt. It was similarly done at the Seattle Repertory Company in February, 1982, directed by Daniel Sullivan.

Its first full production opened at the Cape Playhouse in Dennis, Massachusetts, on August 9, 1982, with the following cast:

CHARLIE	Mark Arnott
TED	Tod Waring
GRACE	Barbara Feldon
ELSIE	Ellen Parker
BONNY	Eve Bennett-Gordon
ANNA TRUMBULL	Eileen Heckart

Melvin Bernhardt was the director, Loren Sherman the designer, Scott Lehrer did the sound, and Denise Romano the costumes. James B. McKenzie was the Executive Producer, Jack V. Booch, the Artistic Producer.

It opened in New York at the Circle Repertory Company on February 6, 1983, with the following cast:

CHARLIE	Ben Siegler
TED	Robert Joy
GRACE	Debra Mooney
ELSIE	Christine Estabrook
BONNY	Ann McDonough
ANNA TRUMBULL	Jacqueline Brookes

John Lee Beatty designed the set, Jennifer Von Mayrhauser the costumes, Craig Miller the lighting, and Chuck London the sound. The production stage manager was Suzanne Fry.

Cast:

Charlie, fourteen*
Ted, sixteen, Charlie's friend*
Grace, Charlie's mother
Elsie, nineteen, Charlie's sister*
Bonny, fourteen*
Anna Trumbull

Time: Summer, 1945

Place: A summer "colony" on the Canadian shore of Lake Erie, near Buffalo, New York.

Set: Simple and presentational. Wooden and wicker furniture, sun-bleached and sandworn, as indicated in ground-plan; a simple wooden glider might serve as a central element, becoming occasionally the front seat of a car. Plenty of sunlight, blue sky, and occasional green shade.

Props: As indicated. In other words, only when it seems simpler to use them than not. For example, the clay in Act I probably is helpful, but plates and glasses for the supper scene probably are not.

Costumes: To be changed or adjusted only when indicated.

*Casting: The young people in this play may be played by actors older than these indicated ages. In this way, we will have more of the sense of actors enacting their roles. Indeed, throughout this play, we should be aware of things in the process of being fabricated or made: the characters by actors; the setting by the manipulation of simple scenic elements; the play itself by its obviously traditional and presentational form.

WHAT I DID LAST SUMMER

ACT ONE

Before Curtain: Music: an old Bing Crosby recording such as "Swinging on a Star." Charlie comes in in khakis, T-shirt, and old sneakers, as a fourteen-year-old.

CHARLIE. (*To audience.*) This is a play about me when I was fourteen, back during the war, when we had this house at a place called Rose Hill, on the Canadian shore of Lake Erie, near Buffalo, New York, where I was born . . . That was the summer I planned to sit around the house . . . (*He sits.*) And study Latin, which I flunked in June . . . and sail my dad's catboat in the races every Wednesday and Saturday . . . or practice driving my mother's car in the driveway . . . (*The bench might momentarily become a car. He mimes driving.*) or play tennis on the Wilsons' clay court . . . (*He is up by now, miming an elaborate serve.*) Pow! and then after a game, me and my friend Ted Moffatt . . . (*Ted runs across the stage, in old clothes.*)
TED. Bombs away! (*He exits* D.R., *whistling like a bomb.*)
CHARLIE. (*Watching him.*) . . . would run down the bank to the beach, jumping over the patches of poison ivy, and then dash over the hot sand, and charge through the water out to the sandbar, where you could dive in, and open your mouth, and drink in half the lake, if you wanted to!
TED. (*Shouting, from Off.*) Come on, Charlie!
CHARLIE. (*Starting to take off his sneakers.*) Prepare to attack! Look out below! (*Grace comes On from* U.L.)
GRACE. Charlie, you stay right where you are! (*She is in her late thirties, attractive, in a simple summer dress.*) Nobody's going near

that water until they've picked up their room! It's an absolute pigsty!
CHARLIE. (*Holding his sneakers.*) Later, Mom.
GRACE. Right now, Charlie!
TED. (*Offstage.*) Zowie! The water's great!
CHARLIE. Mom, Ted's *waiting!* (*He dashes Off, dropping his sneakers Onstage.*)
GRACE. Charlie, I'm warning you . . . Charlie, I am issuing an ultimatum! . . . Charlie! (*But he's gone. Elsie, Charlie's sister, come On from* U.L. *She is nineteen, wears rolled-up blue jeans and a baggy man's shirt. She carries a large copy of "War and Peace."*)
ELSIE. He wouldn't get away with that if Daddy were here.
GRACE. Well Daddy's not here, as we all well know, and so we'll just have to do the best we can without him . . . (*She peers out at the lake.*) Oh now honestly.
ELSIE. What?
GRACE. (*Peering.*) Are those boys . . . wearing . . . their bathing suits?
ELSIE. (*Looking out.*) Oh God.
GRACE. Are they? Or not. I can't tell. (*She shades her eyes.*)
ELSIE. Wouldn't you know.
GRACE. What?
ELSIE. They're playing "When the Moon Comes Over the Mountain."
GRACE. They're playing what?
ELSIE. They're *mooning*, Mother. They think it's an absolute riot. They take everything off, and roll their rear ends around in the waves.
GRACE. Oh don't be silly.
ELSIE. They *do*, Mother. Wait, I'll get the binoculars.
GRACE. That's not necessary, Elsie. (*She stares out.*) Why on earth would they want to do a thing like that?
ELSIE. They like to tease the baby-sitters on the beach. Who think it's a perfect scream.
GRACE. Well I don't think it's funny at all.
ELSIE. Neither do I, Mother. And lately do you know what else they've been doing?
GRACE. I'm not interested, thank you. (*She starts to pick up the sneakers, stops.*) What?
ELSIE. They fill their athletic supporters full of stones, and

then march up and down. All the way to the public beach. With these great bulges in their fronts.

GRACE. Oh honestly.

ELSIE. That's what they do! And it's repulsive, Mother. With women and children around? No one even knows where to look.

GRACE. I'll speak to him.

ELSIE. And here it is just the beginning of summer. Lord knows what he'll be up to by Labor Day. (*She settles down to read "War and Peace" in the chair.*)

GRACE. We'll just have to think up some projects for him, that's all. We'll have to make a good, long list. Repairing the steps, painting the terrace furniture . . .

ELSIE. Oh God, I can see it now. Paint dripping all over the house . . .

GRACE. Now that's enough, Elsie. I don't see you killing yourself this summer.

ELSIE. Mother!

GRACE. And I think *your* room could stand a little more attention.

ELSIE. Mother, I am busy all the *time*. I'm collecting money for Bundles for Britain, I've started *War and Peace* for summer reading. . . .

GRACE. Well all I know is I don't get much help with the errands.

ELSIE. That's because I can't *drive*, Mother.

GRACE. You *can* drive, Elsie. You've even got your license. You just won't, that's all.

ELSIE. I get nervous, Mother.

GRACE. Well you're not too nervous to pick on your brother every other minute.

ELSIE. But he's so imma*ture*, Mother.

GRACE. Yes well, we all have a little growing to do, now don't we.

ELSIE. Oh, Mother, what a snide thing to say!

GRACE. Yes well . . .

ELSIE. I mean it! I just wish Daddy were here, that's all! That's all I wish! (*She storms Off* U.L.)

GRACE. (*Looking after her with a sigh.*) So do I. Oh boy. So do I. (*She picks up Charlie's sneakers as she speaks to the audience.*) This is also a play about me, trying to run a house, trying to run two houses, one here, one in town, trying to keep things clean, trying to keep things going, trying to give two children a good healthy summer, away from the city, away from the polio scare, even during the war, with gas coupons, and meat rationing, and you name it, while my husband is away, overseas for eighteen and a half months, somewhere in the Pacific, cooped up on a destroyer escort, when any minute some Kamikaze pilot could dive down and blow him to smithereens! . . . *that's* what this play is about, if you ask me! And if it isn't, it should be. (*Grace strides Off,* U.L., *carrying Charlie's sneakers, as Charlie and Ted come On from* D.R., *snapping towels at each other, as if they were duellists in a movie. They duel all over the stage, peppering their attacks with expressions from comic books.*)

CHARLIE. Shazam!
TED. Pow!
CHARLIE. Ooof!
TED. Whammo!
CHARLIE. Banzai!
TED. Die, Yankee dog!
CHARLIE. Take that . . . and that . . . and that, you Canuck bastard! (*Ted, suddenly serious, grabs Charlie's towel.*)
TED. What did you say?
CHARLIE. I just said—
TED. You called me a Canuck.
CHARLIE. What's wrong with that? You're Canadian, aren't you?
TED. (*Shoving him.*) I'm not a Canuck, Charlie!
CHARLIE. (*Shoving him back.*) Hey now watch it . . . (*And suddenly they are wrestling in earnest, puffing and grunting. Ted forces Charlie to the ground, and tries to pin him. Charlie writhes and heaves to get out from under. Bonny comes On quickly from* U.L. *She is pretty and young, wearing an informal summer dress.*)
BONNY. Oh *no*! What *now*? (*The boys continue to struggle.*) I thought you two were best friends!
TED. Not when he insults a guy.
CHARLIE. (*Still struggling.*) He can't even take a joke!
BONNY. Let him UP, Ted. He's younger.
TED. First he's got to apologize.
CHARLIE. (*Struggling.*) That'll be the day.

BONNY. Oh you're both so juvenile!
TED. (*Trying to pin him.*) Come on, Charlie, unconditional surrender!
CHARLIE. Never! You Canuck! (*More intense struggling.*)
BONNY. (*Sitting down.*) All right. I just wanted to know who could crew for me this afternoon. (*The boys stop fighting and look at her.*) My father's playing golf, so I get to skipper the Snipe. (*Ted and Charlie jump up.*)
TED & CHARLIE. (*Simultaneously.*) I'll do it . . . Let me . . .
BONNY. (*To Ted.*) I thought you had to cut people's grass this summer, Ted. I thought you had a job.
TED. I'll take the afternoon off.
BONNY. You will?
CHARLIE. Yeah, but I know more about sailing. My dad taught me.
BONNY. That's true. Oh help. I'm terrible about making decisions. Hmmm. (*She makes the most of the moment.*) Tell you what . . . This time I'll take Ted.
CHARLIE. How *come*?
BONNY. Because he's a working man, Charlie. You're free any time, all summer.
CHARLIE. I'm not. I'm working. I work, too.
TED. Yeah sure. For your mother.
CHARLIE. Well you work for your father.
BONNY. It's not the same thing, Charlie. Ted is personally responsible for a large number of lawns.
CHARLIE. That's because his father is caretaker around here. He gave him the job.
TED. I'd better go check out with him, by the way. (*He starts Off,* D.L.)
CHARLIE. (*Calling after him.*) If my dad were home, I'd have a regular job, too. In the city, maybe. We'd drive in together every day. We'd commute!
TED. (*Returning.*) Hey, Charlie, why don't you get a job with the Pig Woman? She's got a notice up in Brodie's drugstore.
CHARLIE. Maybe I will.
TED. I hear she doesn't wear any underpants. Might give you a charge.
BONNY. Don't get grubby, please.

CHARLIE. Maybe I will work for her.
TED. Sure. Work for the Pig Woman. Of course, I hear she pays peanuts. Or maybe it's acorns. (*He goes Off laughing.*)
BONNY. Ted's getting very sarcastic this summer.
CHARLIE. Does the Pig Woman really have a notice up in Brodie's?
BONNY. I don't know, Charlie. You shouldn't work for her anyway. (*They sit down, side by side, on the glider.*)
CHARLIE. Why not?
BONNY. My mother says she's an immoral woman.
CHARLIE. What do you mean, immoral?
BONNY. She used to be somebody's mistress.
CHARLIE. No kidding.
BONNY. She *was*! She was the mistress of some doctor. He kept his wife in town, and brought the Pig Woman out here. And left her that place when he died.
CHARLIE. Ted says she's part Indian.
BONNY. She is! She's got mixed blood. And she's an artist manquée.
CHARLIE. A what?
BONNY. Artist manquée. It means she gives art lessons but nobody takes them.
CHARLIE. Then how can she pay? I mean, if I decide to work for her.
BONNY. I don't know, Charlie. Mother says she's just hanging on, with no visible means of support. (*She gets up.*) And now I've got to go sail. (*She starts Off,* R.)
CHARLIE. (*Getting up.*) Yeah well thanks a bunch for picking Ted.
BONNY. I tried to be fair, Charlie.
CHARLIE. Yeah fair. Uh huh fair. You didn't even let us draw lots.
BONNY. He has a *job*, Charlie. He needs rest and recreation.
CHARLIE. I think you picked him because he's got his driver's license.
BONNY. Oh stop it.
CHARLIE. I do. I think you want to neck with him. In his car.
BONNY. Oh just grow UP, Charlie. Please! (*She goes Off,* U.R.)
CHARLIE. (*Shouting after her.*) That's what I *think*, Bonny. (*Elsie comes On from* U.L. *carrying her "War and Peace."*)

ELSIE. Charlie, Mother's driving to the village, and she needs someone to help with the groceries. (*She takes his towel from him.*)
CHARLIE. Why don't you go?
ELSIE. Because I've made other PLANS, Charlie. (*She spreads the towel out on the platform,* D.R., *and lies down.*) Now hurry! She's waiting in the car! (*Charlie starts shuffling Off.*) God, you're a slob.
CHARLIE. (*Turning, giving her the finger.*) Perch and rotate, Elsie. Perch, and systematically rotate, please. (*He goes Off,* U.L.)
ELSIE. Oh Jesus, you're disgusting. (*The lights dim on Elsie reading, as Grace comes on from* U.R., *briskly, carrying a paper bag. She stops, looks over her shoulder.*)
GRACE. (*To audience.*) *Now* where'd he go? I left him right by the cash register. (*Charlie comes On from* U.R., *carrying another grocery bag.*)
CHARLIE. I dropped the eggs.
GRACE. Oh, Charlie.
CHARLIE. It's O.K. They gave me more.
GRACE. Well let's get things into this car before the ice cream melts. (*They unload the groceries into the "trunk" of the glider.*) Where'd you go earlier? I thought you wanted to pick out the cookies.
CHARLIE. I just went to Brodie's, Mom.
GRACE. To read the funny books?
CHARLIE. No, not to read the "funny" books, Mom. I don't read "funny" books any more.
GRACE. Then what was that I found under your bed?
CHARLIE. That was Classic *Comics,* Mom. For school. A *Tale of Two Cities.*
GRACE. Well I don't consider it a tale of two anything. I threw it out.
CHARLIE. Oh boy. You would. (*They close the "trunk," come around either side, to get into the "car." They talk over the "top."*)
GRACE. Did you at least stop by the post office?
CHARLIE. Of course.
GRACE. Anything?
CHARLIE. I would have told you, Mom.
GRACE. Oh dear.
CHARLIE. It's been five weeks since we heard.
GRACE. Oh well now we mustn't brood. He's on a ship. You wait. Soon there'll be a great stack of letters. For all of us. (*They*

get into the "car." Grace sits for a moment before starting it.) I have a bone to pick with you.
CHARLIE. What?
GRACE. When Mr. McAlister came up by the cash register, you were very rude.
CHARLIE. Who? Boris?
GRACE. Mr. McAlister to you, please.
CHARLIE. He looks like Boris. Of Karloff fame.
GRACE. Well for your information, he happens to be one of the most attractive men in Buffalo.
CHARLIE. He's always hanging around you.
GRACE. Don't be silly.
CHARLIE. He is. He's always coming up.
GRACE. He's a very lonely man.
CHARLIE. Yeah yeah.
GRACE. You just don't know, Charlie. His son was killed in Italy. His wife is in the hospital with a nervous breakdown—
CHARLIE. Well all I know is he's all over you like a tent.
GRACE. Oh, Charlie . . .
CHARLIE. He's a son of a beech . . . (*Grace wheels on him.*) . . . nut tree. (*Grace starts the "car," and mimes driving, very simply. No gear-shifting or foot-pedaling is necessary. Using the "wheel" should be enough. The glider might rock back and forth very simply.*) By the way, I might get a job this summer.
GRACE. We'll think up plenty of jobs.
CHARLIE. I mean a real job.
GRACE. We'll think up a big project.
CHARLIE. I don't mean working for my mother.
GRACE. What did you have in mind then, Charlie?
CHARLIE. There's a notice on Brodie's bulletin board: "Man wanted. Odd Jobs."
GRACE. All right. Try that. Where?
CHARLIE. Black Point.
GRACE. How will you get there? With gas rationing? I can't chauffeur you all over the lakeshore.
CHARLIE. I'll ride my bike.
GRACE. Now that's good, Charlie. That's very enterprising. Daddy would be proud. (*They drive.*) Whom will you be working for, by the way?
CHARLIE. Huh?

GRACE. Don't say "huh," Charlie. Cavemen say "huh."
CHARLIE. I didn't hear your question, Mother dear.
GRACE. I said, whom will you be working for?
CHARLIE. The Pig Woman.
GRACE. Who?
CHARLIE. Anna Trumbull. The Pig Woman. It's her notice up in Brodie's. (*Pause.*)
GRACE. I don't think so, Charlie.
CHARLIE. Why not?
GRACE. I don't think that's a good idea. At all.
CHARLIE. Would you mind telling me why the hell not?
GRACE. Don't swear, please, Charlie. (*Pause.*) She's a disturbing woman, that's why.
CHARLIE. What d'ya mean, disturbing?
GRACE. She's unsettling, Charlie. She likes to rock the boat. Like some other people I know.
CHARLIE. It's a job, Mom!
GRACE. Charlie, you flunked Latin. You have to tutor Latin every Tuesday.
CHARLIE. I'll do that, too!
GRACE. Well, the answer is No, Charlie. N.O. And that's final. (*She looks out.*) Oh look. Look at the corn. It's not as high as an elephant's eye, but I'll bet we'll be having corn on the cob before you know it.
CHARLIE. Big deal.
GRACE. Your favorite thing. Mmmm. Yummy.
CHARLIE. Goodie goodie gum-drop, rah-rah. (*She glances at him. They drive for a moment in silence. Finally.*) Can I drive? Can I at least do that?
GRACE. No you may not.
CHARLIE. Why not?
GRACE. Because it's against the law, Charlie.
CHARLIE. Ted drives.
GRACE. Well he shouldn't.
CHARLIE. Well he does.
GRACE. Well that's because he's Canadian. They do things differently . . . (*She looks out.*) There are the Robinsons. Wave to the Robinsons! Hi, hi! (*She waves as they go by. Charlie gives them the finger out his window.*)
CHARLIE. It's just back roads, Mom.

GRACE. I don't care if it's back roads or Delaware Avenue.
CHARLIE. I've been practicing in our driveway.
GRACE. That's not the open highway.
CHARLIE. Please, Mom.
GRACE. I'm sorry.
CHARLIE. You never let me do anything.
GRACE. I don't let you kill yourself, no.
CHARLIE. You wouldn't even let me have a beer at the Potters'.
GRACE. Not at fourteen, no.
CHARLIE. You're a real wet blanket, Mom. All the time.
GRACE. Who took you and your friends to the movies, just the other night?
CHARLIE. Took us. TOOK us. You wouldn't even let us hitchhike.
GRACE. Not at night. No.
CHARLIE. And we had to see *your* movie. We had to see *Mrs. Miniver* again, for Chrissake.
GRACE. I've asked you not to swear, please.
CHARLIE. (*Softly, out the window.*) Yeah well go to hell. (*Grace slams on the "brakes." They both rock suddenly forward.*)
GRACE. What did you say?
CHARLIE. Never mind.
GRACE. What did you *say*?
CHARLIE. (*Grimly.*) I said "Go to hell."
GRACE. Out of the car.
CHARLIE. Oh, Mom . . .
GRACE. Out. Right now. People who swear at their mothers can learn to walk the rest of the way home.
CHARLIE. I was just—
GRACE. OUT, Charlie. Right now. I mean it. (*She leans grimly across him, and opens his "door." Charlie groans, gets out of the "car," slams the door, walks a little way off. Grace starts the car forward. Charlie fades* U. *She stops the car, and sits for a moment, staring ahead. Charlie watches her. She relents, calls to him, opens the door.*) Come on. (*Charlie approaches the "car" sullenly, and gets back in, closing the "door." Grace starts the "car" forward. Finally.*) Honestly, Charlie, I'm at the end of my rope. I miss Daddy so much, I'm trying so hard to keep things going, and the last thing I need is you being rude to my friends or swearing at me in the car.
CHARLIE. I didn't—

GRACE. You did, Charlie. And you're not much help around the house, either. You leave your breakfast dishes all over the kitchen, and you use twice as much butter as you're supposed to, and I find damp, sandy towels all over your bedroom floor. And I notice that Hitchcock chair by your bed is broken again.
CHARLIE. I'll fix it, Mom.
GRACE. You can't, Charlie. And you can't fix that sugar bowl you broke either. There are special men who do that, and they're all away in the war . . . Well anyway . . . (*She pulls up.*) Here we are. (*She turns, looks at him.*) I'm just asking you to be more helpful, Charlie.
CHARLIE. O.K., Mom. (*He starts to get out of the "car."*)
GRACE. Wait, Charlie. One more thing . . . Now this is awkward, but your father is not around, so it's up to me to say it . . . If ever you have . . . an accident at night, Charlie . . . if ever you have what is known as a nocturnal emission, (*Charlie puts a hand in front of his face.*) don't throw the bedsheets over it and pretend that nothing's happened. Change the *sheets*, Charlie. Or tell me. And I'll change them. (*Long pause. He sits, ultimately humiliated.*) Did you hear me, sweetheart?
CHARLIE. Oh . . . My . . . God!
GRACE. I'm sorry, darling, but I thought I should bring it up.
CHARLIE. (*Jumping out of the "car."*) That does it!
GRACE. Oh now . . .
CHARLIE. That really DOES it, Mom! (*He starts Off.*)
GRACE. Where are you going?
CHARLIE. To get a job with the Pig Woman!
GRACE. Oh no you're not!
CHARLIE. Oh yes I am! (*He runs Off.*)
GRACE. (*Calling after him.*) You come back here and unload this car!
CHARLIE. (*From Offstage.*) Let Elsie do it!
GRACE. (*Calling.*) Charlie! (*Elsie, sitting up from her sun-bathing* D.R., *as the lights come on her again.*)
ELSIE. Let Elsie do what?
GRACE. (*Opening the "trunk."*) Help with the groceries, please.
ELSIE. Why can't Charlie?
GRACE. (*Picking up a grocery bag.*) Don't argue, Elsie. Just do it, please. Just do it right now. (*She starts Off. Elsie begins to poke around in the remaining bag.*)

ELSIE. Did you get melon, Mother? I see cookies for Charlie, but I don't see melon for me. How am I supposed to lose weight if you don't even get any melon? (*She looks up, sees that Grace has gone,* U.L. *turns to audience.*) Oh boy. I'll tell you one thing this play is *not* about. It's not about *me.* It's not about how it feels to grow up during a war when all the boys your age are away. And you can't even go visit your friends from college because "this trip isn't really necessary." And it's not about how someone can miss her father terribly, and how she dreams about him at night, and how he taught her to drive a car, and gave her the confidence to do it, and now he's not around, she's scared even to try. So what does she do with her summer? She sits around, and gripes, and reads, and smokes, and argues, and EATS! And turns herself into a big, fat, slobby PIG! (*She starts Off*) That's what this play is not about, if anyone wants to know. (*She goes Off,* U.L. *Lights might change to give a greener and leafier effect.*)
CHARLIE. (*From Off* L.) Hello? (*No answer. He calls louder.*) Anybody here? (*Charlie comes on, from* L.) Hello! (*Anna Trumbull, the Pig Woman, comes on from* U.R., *as if from around the corner of her cottage. She wears an old, paint-spattered smock, sneakers with holes cut in them for her corns, ankle socks falling around them, and a strange bandana on her head. Her hair is cut in bangs, and straight all around. Her skin is swarthy and sunburned. There is no way of telling her age.*)
ANNA. Scram.
CHARLIE. I just want to —
ANNA. Are you one of those boys who threw crabapples at me from the old orchard?
CHARLIE. No!
ANNA. You sure?
CHARLIE. I never hit you.
ANNA. Get off my land.
CHARLIE. I just want to ask you something.
ANNA. The answer is no.
CHARLIE. Wait till I ask!
ANNA. No, I do not have any tin cans for the war effort.
CHARLIE. I'm not collecting tin cans.
ANNA. Then what?
CHARLIE. I read your notice . . . At Brodie's . . . "Man wanted. Odd jobs."
ANNA. Oh that. I put that up in March.

CHARLIE. It's still there.
ANNA. Tell them to take it down.
CHARLIE. You found a man?
ANNA. I did not. There are no men to be found. And where do you think they are? Shooting, maiming, killing each other in all four corners of the globe.
CHARLIE. My father's in the Pacific.
ANNA. I'm sure he is.
CHARLIE. So can I work for you?
ANNA. You?
CHARLIE. Me.
ANNA. What can you do?
CHARLIE. Me?
ANNA. You.
CHARLIE. I can cut your grass.
ANNA. What grass? Do you see any grass around here?
CHARLIE. No.
ANNA. Grass. The very idea galls me. The very notion. Think about grass. Have you ever thought about it?
CHARLIE. No.
ANNA. Then do. Think. Question your assumptions. Think of what grass requires. Think of the topsoil, think of the fertilizer, think of the precious water. Have you ever thought about that?
CHARLIE. No.
ANNA. Have you ever thought of the poor human souls who spend their lives planting it and rolling it and keeping it trim?
CHARLIE. My friend Ted cuts grass.
ANNA. There you are. Think of that.
CHARLIE. I will.
ANNA. And think of the history of grass. Explore its origins. Do you know where it came from?
CHARLIE. No.
ANNA. Grass came directly from the English aristocracy. They thought it up, in order to play their silly games. They bred it and fed it and put signs on it saying keep off it. Got the picture? Wherever there's grass, there's class. Will you remember that? Remember I told you?
CHARLIE. Yes.
ANNA. Good. Then the day's not lost. (*She starts Off* U.R.)
CHARLIE. I could do something else, though.

ANNA. (*Wheeling on him.*) Can you put in plumbing? Can you dig a ditch all the way out to the new sewer line? Can you put in pipes? Can you pay for them?
CHARLIE. No.
ANNA. Can you fix a pump?
CHARLIE. I fixed the fuel pump on our Ford station wagon.
ANNA. I don't care about cars.
CHARLIE. What about that old car I saw in your barn?
ANNA. It doesn't work any more.
CHARLIE. I could try and fix it.
ANNA. I don't want a car. I've learned to get along without one. (*She starts Off* R. *again.*)
CHARLIE. Then I could do something *else.* You could teach me. (*She stops, turns.*)
ANNA. How old are you?
CHARLIE. Sixteen. (*Pause.*) A year from next November.
ANNA. Which means what?
CHARLIE. Fourteen.
ANNA. A babe. A mere babe. Where are you from?
CHARLIE. Up the beach. Rose Hill.
ANNA. A lost boy. From the Fort. Who's wandered into Indian territory . . . Did you know I had Indian blood?
CHARLIE. Yes.
ANNA. My great-grandmother was a Tuscarora Indian princess.
CHARLIE. Oh.
ANNA. My father was vice-president of the Erie County Street Railway Corporation. I'll bet you didn't know that.
CHARLIE. No.
ANNA. Did you know that my cottage was once a pigsty?
CHARLIE. No.
ANNA. Oh yes. That's why they call me the Pig Woman. Do you think it suits me?
CHARLIE. Um . . .
ANNA. Don't answer that. I like the name. It sets me off. It makes me different. Does that frighten you?
CHARLIE. No. (*Pause.*)
ANNA. When could you work?
CHARLIE. Any time. (*Pause.*) Except Wednesday and Satur-

day afternoons.
ANNA. Why not then?
CHARLIE. That's when they have the sailing races.
ANNA. Goodbye.
CHARLIE. I have to. I signed up.
ANNA. I refuse to accommodate myself to the leisure class.
CHARLIE. I'll work every morning for you.
ANNA. Every morning?
CHARLIE. Except Tuesdays.
ANNA. Scram. Vamoose.
CHARLIE. I have to tutor on Tuesdays.
ANNA. Bye-bye.
CHARLIE. I flunked Latin! I have to tutor!
ANNA. Back to Rose Hill! Back to the stockade, white man! (*She goes Off* R.)
CHARLIE. (*Calling after her.*) O.K. I'll work it OUT. I'll quit the sailing, if I can have the job. (*Pause; she comes back on.*)
ANNA. I can see you're willing to make a momentous sacrifice . . . All right. I'll hire you.
CHARLIE. Thanks.
ANNA. I'll give you twenty-five cents an hour.
CHARLIE. Huh?
ANNA. Twenty-five.
CHARLIE. That's all?
ANNA. That's enough for a beginner.
CHARLIE. My friend Ted gets fifty.
ANNA. For what?
CHARLIE. Cutting grass.
ANNA. You see what grass does to the economy?
CHARLIE. I got twenty-five cents two *years* ago just for walking the Watsons' dog.
ANNA. I know that dog. That dog isn't worth a dime.
CHARLIE. Well I just can't work for twenty-five cents an hour. I just can't.
ANNA. Well I just can't afford to pay you anything more. Sorry.
CHARLIE. Which means I got to go back to Rose Hill and tell everybody and his uncle I couldn't get a job, and take a lot of crap from my mother and sister, and listen to Ted sling the bull

all summer, and feel like a baby in front of Bonny! Darn it! Darn it all! Damn it! Goddammit to hell! (*He turns and starts Off* L.)
ANNA. Stop! (*He does.*) Come here! (*He does.*) Let me see your hands.
CHARLIE. (*Stopping.*) My hands?
ANNA. Let me see them. (*Charlie wipes his hands on his pants, then holds them up. Anna crosses, takes them, looks them over.*) You have very expressive hands.
CHARLIE. I do?
ANNA. You also have strong feelings.
CHARLIE. I sure do.
ANNA. (*Dropping his hands.*) Because of your hands, and your feelings, I have decided to give you more than twenty-five cents an hour.
CHARLIE. Hey, thanks.
ANNA. I've decided to give you art lessons.
CHARLIE. Art lessons?
ANNA. I will root out your talent, wherever it lies. I will teach you to express your feelings with your hands.
CHARLIE. Every day?
ANNA. Every afternoon. And what you will get from me will be worth far more than money. Now make up your mind. Work here on these terms, or run back to Rose Hill and tell them you turned down a chance to build your body and stretch your soul with Anna Trumbull, the Pig Woman.
CHARLIE. (*Finally.*) I'll do it. (*She sits, indicates that he is to sit beside her.*)
ANNA. Good. You will arrive every morning at eight o'clock. I'll probably be asleep. Walk right in and give me a good shake. I sleep soundly because I have such delicious dreams. My lover, old Doctor Holloway, used to wake me with a kiss. No need for you to do that. Just hand me a cup of strong, hot coffee, and then we will proceed to labor in the vineyards together.
CHARLIE. O.K.
ANNA. We will work primarily out of doors, in the soil, in the sun. At noon, we will swim off the rocks in my cove. Bring your bathing suit or not, as you see fit. I don't wear one myself. I find them inhibiting. Do you?
CHARLIE. Um . . .

ANNA. Never mind. It's not important. After our swim we will have lunch. I will provide it. It will consist of homemade bread, unprocessed cheese, and fruit in season. And one glass of good red wine. Do you have any trouble with wine?
CHARLIE. No.
ANNA. I do. Because of my Indian blood, I have a weakness for alcohol. I hope you'll keep an eye on me in that department.
CHARLIE. O.K.
ANNA. Good. And while we eat, we will sit in the shade and talk. I will tell you about town. I grew up there, and think of it with all the passion of an exile. Would you like to hear me rail against your homeland?
CHARLIE. Sure.
ANNA. Then you've come to the right place . . . But in the afternoon, we will get serious. We will create things together. We will seek patterns, we will make shapes, we will fabricate visions of a better world. Is that all clear?
CHARLIE. Yes, Miss Trumbull.
ANNA. Call me Anna, since we are to be colleagues in life and art. (*They get up.*)
CHARLIE. O.K., Anna.
ANNA. And what do I call you?
CHARLIE. Charlie. Charlie Higgins.
ANNA. Higgins. I knew the Higgins family. Stuffy bunch, all the way down the line. Loved money, hated horses, never knew what to do about women.
CHARLIE. That's me.
ANNA. One of them married a girl named Grace Anderson.
CHARLIE. That's my mom.
ANNA. No!
CHARLIE. Sure. She's my mother.
ANNA. (*Bursting into laughter.*) Oh boy. Ohboyohboyohboyohboy. That's a pip. That's a lulu. The chickens come home to roost. Does she know you're here?
CHARLIE. Sort of.
ANNA. "Sort of." I'll bet "sort of." (*She laughs again.*) Well we'll see you tomorrow, Charlie. *If* we see you tomorrow. (*She goes Off* R., *laughing, shaking her head. Charlie stands looking after her, then goes Off slowly in the opposite direction, as Bonny comes out from* U.R., *carrying a towel, calling Offstage as she enters.*)

BONNY. All right! It's an hour after lunch! Everybody can go in the water! (*Bonny spreads the towel, as if she were on a beach. She speaks quietly to the audience.*) Sometimes I think this play is secretly about me. That's what I secretly think. Because, for me, this is a crucial summer. All sorts of important things are beginning to happen. My father's letting me skipper the boat occasionally. And my mother says I can smoke, as long as it's in front of her. And I've got a paid baby-sitting job three times a week. (*She calls out.*) It's not cold, Susie. Just go in slowly. Bit by bit. And it'll feel fine. (*To audience.*) And tonight, one of the most crucial things of all might happen. Tonight we might be riding this roller coaster. It's called The Cyclone, and on a calm night you can hear it roar, even though the amusement park is over five miles away! Oh it's the scariest thing! It's built right out over the lake, all rickety and shaky, and they say when you climb to the top, you can see all the way to town. And when you start down, it's so basically terrifying that *women* have thrown their *babies* over the *side*! It costs five tickets per person per ride, and there's a big sign right at the gate saying you have to be at least sixteen before you can ride it. But Ted knows the Canadian boys who take tickets, and right now he's seeing if they can sneak us on. (*Calls out.*) Nobody goes out beyond the sandbar, please! Stay in the shallow water where I can see you! (*Ted comes on eagerly, from* U.L.)
TED. Everything's copasetic.
BONNY. They'll let us on.
TED. No problem.
BONNY. Oh I'm shaking like a leaf. Did you tell Charlie?
TED. How could I tell Charlie? He's over at the Pig Woman's again.
BONNY. We'll have to wait and see if he can come too.
TED. Why Charlie?
BONNY. Because last summer we all promised to ride it together.
TED. They won't let him on. He's too young.
BONNY. He's my age.
TED. That's different. I told them you were my girl.
BONNY. Your *girl*?
TED. So they'd let you through.
BONNY. You mean you didn't mention Charlie?

TED. I said I was bringing my girl.
BONNY. Oh. (*She calls out.*) Stay together, everybody! Everybody stay close together! (*Pause.*)
TED. So what do you say?
BONNY. How would we get there?
TED. How do you think? By car.
BONNY. With you driving? Or your father?
TED. I got my license, remember?
BONNY. I can't, then.
TED. How come?
BONNY. My mother doesn't want me to go out alone at night in cars with older boys. She was even mad I took you sailing with me.
TED. That wasn't a car. And it wasn't at night.
BONNY. Well I don't know. She thinks you're too old for me.
TED. She didn't think that last summer.
BONNY. Well maybe you weren't last summer. (*Calling out.*) Yes I saw, Susie! I saw you do that somersault! That was very good, Susie.
TED. Don't tell her then.
BONNY. Don't *tell* her?
TED. Just meet me out by the main road.
BONNY. Without Charlie?
TED. Look, Charlie's going his way, why can't we go ours? Come on. I'll fix it so we ride in the front row. And I'll take you to the Frozen Custard place afterwards. And introduce you to my whole gang from high school.
BONNY. Gosh . . .
TED. (*Touching her arm.*) Sure. It'll be like a date. A real date.
BONNY. You're distracting me, Ted. I'm supposed to be watching these . . . (*She looks out at the lake.*) . . . kids. (*She jumps to her feet.*) Uh-oh.
TED. What?
BONNY. How many heads do you see out there?
TED. (*Counting quickly.*) One . . . two . . . three . . . four . . .
BONNY. There's supposed to be five!
TED. (*Pointing.*) And five, over there!
BONNY. Thank God! (*Calling out angrily.*) Susie, when you decide to swim underwater, would you *tell* people, please?
TED. Close call, huh?

BONNY. That wouldn't have happened if I had used the buddy system.
TED. I hate the buddy system.
BONNY. Well at least it's safe. (*Clapping her hands.*) Everyone out of the water, please. I'm instigating a new rule! (*She starts Off* U.R.)
TED. What about our date?
BONNY. Tell you what: I'll ask my father.
TED. He'll say no.
BONNY. He might not. He lets me do more than my mother. (*She goes Off* U.R.) New rule, everybody! New rule! We're going to have the buddy system! (*She goes Off.*)
TED. (*Calling after her.*) Your father will say no! (*To audience.*) Sure he'll say no. Lookit, someday somebody ought to write a play about a Canadian kid who hangs around Americans while his dad takes care of their summer homes. Here's the story: First, he's friends with those kids, trading comics with them, playing tennis, horsing around on the raft. Everything's hunky-dory. Then he starts growing hair on his nuts, and what do you know? The plot thickens. Suddenly when he shows up at the tennis courts, he gets the fish-eye from Mrs. Putnam for even sitting down and watching, for Christ sake. And soon he feels creepy even going down to the beach, like now it's out of bounds, or something. And then suppose he wants to take out an American girl. My God, suddenly it's like he wants to French kiss her, and bang her, and carry her off to Saskatchewan, all on the first date! I dunno. All I know is somebody ought to write about it some time. (*Elsie comes on from* L. *and begins to organize the chairs* C., *and stools* L. *and* R., *for supper. Grace comes on from* R., *and helps. No actual table is necessary.*)
ELSIE. Where've you been?
GRACE. Oh, just having a quick drink with poor Mr. McAlister.
ELSIE. Did you ask him what to do about Charlie?
GRACE. I did not. Charlie is our problem, and we can deal with it by ourselves.
ELSIE. Where is he now, by the way?
GRACE. Out by the hose. Washing his hands. Which were covered with purple paint.
ELSIE. Purple?

GRACE. Don't ask *me* what she has him doing.
ELSIE. I hope you let him have it, Mother. Tonight I hope you read him the riot act. He's been late for dinner ever since he started that stupid job.
GRACE. Sssshhh.
ELSIE. And he's missed two turns to set the table.
GRACE. He'll make it up.
ELSIE. And he ruins the meal, Mother. With all those obnoxious ideas she gives him.
GRACE. Sshh. We have ideas, too. We'll just have to counteract them. (*They sit down, Grace in the chair, C., Elsie on the stool, R.*)
ELSIE. Well I hope tonight you make him do the dishes, at least. Including the pots and pans. Otherwise it isn't fair.
GRACE. Ssshh. (*She hears him coming.*) We're just going to have to hold the line, Elsie. As the Marines did on Iwo Jima. Now are we allies in this, or not?
ELSIE. We're allies, Mother.
GRACE. Thank you, dear. (*They shake hands. Charlie enters from up R.*) Good evening, Charlie.
CHARLIE. (*Very jauntily.*) Hi.
GRACE. Sit down, dear.
CHARLIE. O.K. (*He sits on stool, L.*)
GRACE. Pour Charlie some milk, please, Elsie. (*Elsie "pours milk" with grim reluctance.*)
CHARLIE. Thanks.
GRACE. (*Serving "food."*) Now, Charlie, am I giving you too much cauliflower? Speak now, or forever hold your peace. (*She hands him a "plate"; little pantomiming of eating is necessary.*)
CHARLIE. What's this other stuff?
GRACE. Chicken croquettes, dear. (*Charlie makes a loud barfing sound.*) Now that's enough, please.
CHARLIE. You know what they look like, don't you?
GRACE. We're not interested, Charlie.
ELSIE. We're not interested.
CHARLIE. Dog turds left on the beach.
ELSIE. Make him leave the table, Mother.
GRACE. I'll handle this, Elsie. (*Smiling, to Charlie.*) Somebody's feeling his oats a little these days. Am I right? Somebody is full of beans these days.
CHARLIE. Maybe.

GRACE. Otherwise you would not have made such an unattractive remark about the food. Which we are lucky to have. Which millions of refugees throughout Europe would give their eye-*teeth* for.

CHARLIE. Send it to 'em.

ELSIE. Brat.

CHARLIE. (*To Elsie.*) Wrap it up, and put it in a Bundle for Britain.

ELSIE. Will you shut *up*?

GRACE. Now stop it, both of you. (*Pause.*) I take it you enjoy your new job, Charlie.

CHARLIE. Uh huh.

GRACE. You must, because it seems to occupy so much of your time.

CHARLIE. Uh huh.

GRACE. For example, I hear you missed your Latin lesson last Tuesday.

CHARLIE. Oh yeah.

GRACE. Missed it completely. Without even telephoning Mrs. Blackburn to cancel it.

CHARLIE. Sorry.

GRACE. Even after you promised Daddy you'd study it all summer long.

CHARLIE. I said I was sorry.

GRACE. Even though you might have to stay behind a grade if you don't pass it in the fall.

CHARLIE. I'm studying it on my own.

ELSIE. You haven't cracked a book.

CHARLIE. Well you know why, don't you?

ELSIE. No, why?

CHARLIE. Latin is the language of the leisure class.

GRACE. What?

CHARLIE. It's true. We all study Latin just because the poor people don't have time to.

ELSIE. Oh my God.

GRACE. That is a silly argument, Charlie, and I think I know where it came from.

CHARLIE. Well it's true, anyway.

GRACE. It is not true. Latin is . . . (*Charlie and Elsie look at her*

expectantly.) Latin is the basic building block of western civilization. And I don't think we need to discuss it any further.
ELSIE. Thank God.
GRACE. What is she paying you, by the way?
CHARLIE. I prefer not to say.
GRACE. I'll pay you more.
CHARLIE. To do what?
GRACE. Paint the garage.
CHARLIE. No thanks.
GRACE. I'll pay you twice what she pays you.
CHARLIE. No thanks, Mom.
GRACE. I'll just have to get someone else, then.
CHARLIE. O.K.
GRACE. I'll just have to get your friend Ted Moffatt to come over and paint our garage. For a dollar an hour.
ELSIE. *I'll* do it for that. I'll paint it.
GRACE. Stay *out* of this, Elsie. Please. (*Pause.*) What do you think of her, Charlie?
CHARLIE. Who? Elsie? She's a drip.
GRACE. I'm talking about Miss Trumbull, Charlie.
CHARLIE. Oh, you mean Anna.
GRACE. Yes. All right. Anna. What do you think?
CHARLIE. I like her.
GRACE. You do?
CHARLIE. We get along fine.
GRACE. Does she know who you are, Charlie?
CHARLIE. Who I *am*?
GRACE. Your name? Does she know the name?
CHARLIE. Oh sure.
GRACE. Did it ring a bell?
CHARLIE. What?
GRACE. When you told her your name, what did she say?
CHARLIE. She said she knew you.
ELSIE. Who knew who?
CHARLIE. Anna knew Mom.
ELSIE. What?
GRACE. Oh heavens. Years ago. For a short time. I took an art class from her.
ELSIE. You never told me that.

CHARLIE. I didn't know you were an artist, Mom.
GRACE. I'm not. Oh I thought I was. I did a few little things with water colors. Flowers and things. But that's not the point, anyway. The point is, Charlie, that when Daddy went to war, you promised to help.
CHARLIE. I will, Mom.
GRACE. Well I don't see you doing it. I don't see you lifting a finger around here since you started that job.
CHARLIE. I'll do it, Mom. I swear. (*He gets up, starts to take his "plate" Off* L.)
GRACE. You haven't even cut the grass.
CHARLIE. (*Wheeling on her.*) I don't believe in grass.
ELSIE. Oh my God!
CHARLIE. Have you ever questioned your assumptions about grass?
ELSIE. Have you ever questioned your assumptions about setting the table?
GRACE. Now stop it!
CHARLIE. We should plow that lawn up! We should use it for growing vegetables! We should fertilize it with our own wastes!
ELSIE. See, Mother, how repulsive he is!
GRACE. Charlie, that's enough! Now all I know is you can't do all the things you have to do for me, and still work for Anna Trumbull!
CHARLIE. You mean, quit?
GRACE. That's what I mean.
CHARLIE. But I like her.
GRACE. Charlie, I am asking you, as a special favor, if not for me, then for your father, to give up that job. Will you, Charlie? For your father? Who's away at war? (*Charlie looks at her, then goes Off* L., *carrying his "plate." Grace asks Elsie.*) What does that mean?
ELSIE. Don't ask me. I only live here.
GRACE. Oh dear.
ELSIE. Some Iwo Jima, Mother.
GRACE. The battle's not over yet, Elsie. (*Charlie comes back in and sits down.*)
CHARLIE. What's for dessert?
GRACE. I'll tell you when I hear your answer, Charlie.
CHARLIE. The answer is no.

GRACE. I am asking you, please.
CHARLIE. No!
GRACE. All right, Charlie, then from here on in, unless you want real trouble, I expect your room to be immaculate, and the chores done thoroughly, and a new chapter of Latin learned every single day! And if Miss Trumbull complains about your time, you tell her that your first responsibility is to your family.
CHARLIE. She says my first responsibility is to myself!
GRACE. Well she's wrong.
CHARLIE. She says the family is a dying social unit!
GRACE. She is just plain wrong!
CHARLIE. She says family pressure causes half the misery in the world, and you ought to know it more than anyone!
GRACE. Well you tell her . . . You tell her from me . . . (*Pause.*) Oh honestly — (*She throws down her "napkin," turns, and strides Off,* U.L. *Pause.*)
ELSIE. Now you've done it. I hope she sits down and writes Daddy a long letter. All about you!
CHARLIE. Oh gee.
ELSIE. She made the dessert especially for you, too. Cookie pudding. With whipped cream.
CHARLIE. Oh God, what'll I do?
ELSIE. First you better do those dishes, Charlie.
CHARLIE. O.K.
ELSIE. Including the pots and pans.
CHARLIE. O.K., O.K.
ELSIE. And then you better go up and knock on her door and apologize. The way Daddy used to do.
CHARLIE. O.K.
ELSIE. And you better have your Latin book right in your hand.
CHARLIE. Good idea.
ELSIE. And you better say you're quitting the Pig Woman!
CHARLIE. Never!
ELSIE. Then God help us all! (*She goes Off, as the lights change to Anna's mottled world. She comes on from* U.R., *carrying an old galvanized tub.*)
ANNA. (*Calling to Charlie.*) Look what I got from the lake.
CHARLIE. (*Leaving the table, moving the chair.*) I fixed your chair, Anna!

ANNA. Good! All the more reason to look here. (*She places the tub on something, and regards it reverently.*) What do you think this is?
CHARLIE. (*Looking in.*) Mud.
ANNA. Mud? It's not mud at all. Clay! Good, thick, red Lake Erie clay! Which I dredged up from under a rock, like an Indian maiden, diving for pearls. (*She sits,* D.R.)
CHARLIE. Oh.
ANNA. Is that all you can say? Just "Oh."
CHARLIE. (*Lying down, stretching.*) I'm kind of tired today, Anna. I had to do extra chores for my mother.
ANNA. That's exactly why I brought you this. Touch it. Feel it. (*Charlie sits up, begins to dip his fingers into the tub, very gingerly at first.*) Go on. Dig in. Get your hands dirty. Squeeze it. Knead it. Make it ooze. (*He tries.*) How does it feel?
CHARLIE. Good.
ANNA. Of course it does. It's the muck of life. It's the primal sludge. Work it around for a while. Perhaps we'll discover you're a sculptor.
CHARLIE. You don't think I'm a painter?
ANNA. I've decided you're not.
CHARLIE. I told you I wasn't.
ANNA. Well you tried. I appreciate that. But last night, I reviewed your entire *oeuvre* since you arrived, and I've decided I don't like it. There was only one drawing which had energy and vitality. And that had to do with airplanes.
CHARLIE. That was a Grumman Wildcat attacking a Japanese Zero over the Coral Sea.
ANNA. Whatever. I put it aside, with the rest. I did not come into this world to encourage young people to portray death and destruction. Try sculpture instead.
CHARLIE. How do you know I'm a sculptor?
ANNA. I know you're something. The problem is simply bringing it out.
CHARLIE. Maybe I'm a mechanic. I wish you'd let me fix your car.
ANNA. Cars come and go. Planes rise and fall. I want you to do something more permanent. . . . Now get at that clay.
CHARLIE. I can't decide what to make.
ANNA. Make a man. Make yourself.
CHARLIE. I don't feel much like a man.

ANNA. Good God, what are you saying?
CHARLIE. I dunno. I flunked Latin, I don't have my driver's license, Bonny treats me like her little brother. Sometimes I think I'll never be a man.
ANNA. Good heavens. Being a man or a woman isn't any of those things. It's simply realizing your potential.
CHARLIE. You think I've got some?
ANNA. I think everyone does. Even Hitler. But most people never find the right way to work it out. And then there's trouble.
CHARLIE. Have you found a way of working out yours?
ANNA. Of course.
CHARLIE. Then how come I never see you making anything?
ANNA. I'm making something right now.
CHARLIE. Huh?
ANNA. Work that clay, please. (*Charlie works the clay; Anna basks in the sun.*)
CHARLIE. Anna?
ANNA. Mmm?
CHARLIE. If I hadn't shown up, would you have looked for another kid?
ANNA. They have to come to me.
CHARLIE. Do lots of people come to you?
ANNA. No. Not many. Some. Your mother did. But she didn't stay.
CHARLIE. Why not?
ANNA. I'm too dangerous.
CHARLIE. Yeah, dangerous. That's a good one, dangerous.
ANNA. I am, Charlie. Because I'm a great teacher. And all great teachers are dangerous. Such as Socrates. Or Christ. Or me.
CHARLIE. Don't be conceited, Anna.
ANNA. Yes well, ask your mother how dangerous I am.
CHARLIE. Oh hell, she thinks even comic books are dangerous.
ANNA. Yes well, keep working.
CHARLIE. (*As he works.*) Maybe next summer, some other kid will come around with more potential.
ANNA. I won't be here next summer.
CHARLIE. Sure you will.
ANNA. Oh no. I've put my ear to the ground, and I hear the cavalry coming.

CHARLIE. What cavalry?
ANNA. Never mind, but they'll be here, Charlie. So you're my last best hope. Now let's see what you've done.
CHARLIE. Not much, actually.
ANNA. It lacks commitment . . . We'll have to liberate your spirit. We'll tune up on my tomatoes.
CHARLIE. Your tomahtoes? Again?
ANNA. My to*may*toes, please. They're a vulgar fruit. Use the vulgar pronunciation.
CHARLIE. We've already talked about your tomaytoes.
ANNA. Then let's see how much you remember.
CHARLIE. Your seeds go way, way back.
ANNA. Yes.
CHARLIE. They came from your great-grandmother who was an Indian princess . . .
ANNA. Yes . . .
CHARLIE. And she got them from her lover, who was a French trapper . . .
ANNA. Yes. Who rowed them across the Niagara gorge . . .
CHARLIE. And so they've come down to you . . .
ANNA. Generation by generation . . .
CHARLIE. (*With more enthusiasm.*) And they'll last beyond you, too . . .
ANNA. Exactly. Because they're perennials. See? All the little buds are beginning. Soon we'll have flowers, and then fruit. Most people do what at this point?
CHARLIE. They pinch them and stake them and prune them.
ANNA. But not me . . .
CHARLIE. You let them grow any way they want . . .
ANNA. And all, all will bear fruit, as long as they get plenty of water, plenty of sun and plenty of . . .
BOTH. Good, honest shit!
ANNA. (*She bends down.*) Here. I'll pinch off a shoot. (*She brings it to him.*) Smell that. Inhale it deep into your lungs . . . Now close your eyes, and keep working . . . (*He does.*) That's the smell of old France, and Canada, and the Niagara Frontier . . . At the end of the summer, I plan to give you some of my seeds. Some day, some other summer, you will have the pleasure of picking a ripe tomato from one of my plants. First, you will simply weigh it in the palm of your hand. Then you will admire

its shape and color. Suddenly you will close your eyes and mash it into your mouth. You'll let the juice spill out, and the meat roll around on your tongue, and then you'll swallow—meat, juice, seeds, and all. And then you'll open your eyes, open them wide, and give out a great, loud war-whoop of praise to life, and the noble tomato, and to me, Anna Trumbull, the Pig Woman, who introduced you to it. (*She crosses to him.*) And now let's see what you've done. (*She takes up his work, looks at it.*) Hmmm.
CHARLIE. It keeps collapsing.
ANNA. Mmmm.
CHARLIE. Maybe I'm not a sculptor either.
ANNA. Of course you are. I'll tell you what you've made. What you've made is a spectacular ash-tray, that's what you've made. If I smoked, I'd use it continuously. In fact, it's so good I'm thinking of taking up smoking.
CHARLIE. You're just trying to make me feel better.
ANNA. Well what's wrong with that? Go wash off in the lake while I fix lunch, and then we'll try again. (*They start Off* R.)
CHARLIE. After lunch, can't I work on your car? Maybe *that's* my potential.
ANNA. Nonsense. After lunch we'll try working with wood.
CHARLIE. Oh Anna . . .
ANNA. And if wood doesn't work, we'll try something else. We'll keep plugging, you and I, on into the night.
CHARLIE. I'm going out with my friends tonight.
ANNA. (*As they exit,* R.) Well then we'll seize the day. And if you work hard, I will tell you the story of my cucumbers. There is an amusing anecdote connecting them to the sexual member of my lover, old Doctor Holloway. I think you're man enough to hear it. (*They exit,* R., *Charlie carrying the tub. Ted comes on from* U.L. *singing "Pistol Packin' Mama." He gets into his "car," adjusts the "mirror," combs his hair, and then waits impatiently. Bonny backs On nervously from* U.L.)
TED. (*Rolling down the "window", leaning out.*) Come on.
BONNY. He's not here yet.
TED. Who? Don't tell me you asked Charlie!
BONNY. He said he'd meet me in the driveway right after supper.
TED. You and your buddy system . . . You'd think a guy could ask a girl for a date without her bringing along another guy.

BONNY. Charlie's not just another guy.
TED. Do you think you could at least wait for him in the car? Or would your dad think you were necking with a Canuck?
BONNY. I can wait in the car, Ted. (*Ted gets out, crosses around the front and opens the door for her. She gets in uneasily. She sneaks a peek in the "mirror" while he crosses back.*)
TED. (*Getting into the "car."*) Did you tell your folks you were going to the Cyclone?
BONNY. I decided not to. I told them we were all going to see *Dumbo*.
TED. "All." I love that "all."
BONNY. They're at least letting me drive in your car, Ted. That's something, at least.
TED. Yeah well, look. Here comes your buddy. (*Charlie comes on from* U.L.)
CHARLIE. Sorry.
TED. Where were you?
CHARLIE. I fell asleep.
TED. Asleep? At eight in the evening?
CHARLIE. I was tired. O.K.? I've been working for two women. (*Charlie starts to get in next to Bonny. Ted reaches behind Bonny, to pull forward the "seat."*)
TED. Get in back, O.K.?
CHARLIE. How come I can't sit in front?
TED. It's a floor gearshift. Get in back.
BONNY. He's just gotten his license, Charlie.
TED. I just want him in back.
BONNY. Be reasonable, Charlie. (*Charlie reluctantly gets into the back, shoving Bonny forward by the "seat." Bonny closes the "door."*)
TED. And we are off. To the Cyclone! (*He starts up the "car."*)
CHARLIE. (*Leaning forward, between them.*) Don't you think you better put on your lights first, Ted?
TED. (*Quickly putting the "lights" on.*) I was planning to do that.
CHARLIE. (*Sitting back.*) Oh yeah. Sure. Right. You bet. (*They drive.*)
TED. So, Charlie. How's the Pig Woman?
CHARLIE. Fine.
TED. Is it true she doesn't wear any underpants?
BONNY. Oh honestly . . .
CHARLIE. No.

TED. No she doesn't? Or no it's not true?
CHARLIE. She wears underwear, Ted.
BONNY. Of course she does.
TED. How do you know, Charlie? Have you looked?
CHARLIE. Knock it off, Ted. O.K.?
BONNY. Yes, Ted. Stop teasing. Really. (*They drive.*)
TED. What does she pay you, Charlie?
CHARLIE. Never mind.
BONNY. My father says it's rude to talk about money.
TED. Hey look. I'm just a poor Canuck who wants to know what the rich Americans are paying their help this summer.
CHARLIE. She's not rich.
TED. That's why she only pays a quarter.
CHARLIE. There are more things in this world than money, Ted.
BONNY. Yes, Ted.
TED. Such as what?
BONNY. Look out for that car! (*Ted swerves. They all lean. Ted straightens the "wheel."*)
CHARLIE. Jesus. Drive much?
TED. I saw him.
CHARLIE. Uh huh. You betchum, Ted.
TED. I want to know what the Pig Woman gives you that's more important than money, Charlie.
CHARLIE. Things you wouldn't understand, Ted.
TED. Such as what? (*Silence from Charlie.*)
BONNY. Such as what, Charlie?
CHARLIE. Whose side are you on, Bonny?
BONNY. I'm just curious, Charlie. What does she give you?
CHARLIE. She . . . teaches me things.
TED. *Teaches* you? You mean, like a . . . *teacher*?
BONNY. What does she teach you, Charlie?
CHARLIE. She . . . I don't have to tell.
TED. You don't have to ride the Cyclone, either. (*He stops the "car." They all jerk forward.*) Maybe we'll just sit here by the side of the road until we hear about those wonderful, secret, piggy things.
BONNY. Oh, Ted.
CHARLIE. Fine with me. Maybe there are more important things than riding some dumb machine in an amusement park.

BONNY. Oh, Charlie.
TED. O.K. We sit.
CHARLIE. You know what amusement parks are, don't you? Amusement parks are places where people fritter away their potential.
TED. Fritter away their what?
CHARLIE. Potential. Potential.
BONNY. What does that mean, Charlie?
CHARLIE. It means that everyone's got this potential, if they only use it right. I've got it, you've got it, Hitler's got it, even Ted's got it.
BONNY. Is that what she teaches you, Charlie?
CHARLIE. Sure. And she's trying to bring mine out.
TED. Yeah well tell her I got some potential right here in my pants.
BONNY. That's disgusting, Ted.
CHARLIE. Yes, Ted. Knock it off. There are ladies present.
TED. Want to make something out of it, Charlie.
BONNY. Oh stop!
TED. Or don't you have enough potential?
CHARLIE. I'll make something out of it, Ted.
TED. O.K., then let's get out of the car, you dumb little creep.
CHARLIE. (*Pushing against Bonny's seat.*) O.K., you crude Canadian townie hick!
TED. (*Leaping out of the "car."*) You'll be gumming your food, buster!
BONNY. Oh God!
CHARLIE. (*Holding his ground.*) I'm not scared of you! (*They square off. Bonny is out of the "car" by now, and comes between them.*)
BONNY. Oh stop! Please! Ted, you're two years older!
CHARLIE. Just a year and a half. (*They face each other. Then Ted backs off.*)
TED. You're lucky there's a woman around, Charlie.
CHARLIE. (*Making his knees shake, like a cartoon character.*) I'm scared, Ted. Help. Gasp. Shriek. (*He starts Off* L.)
BONNY. How will you get home, Charlie?
CHARLIE. Who has to go home? I've got other places to go besides home! (*He runs Off. Bonny returns to the "car." Ted tries to close the "door" for her. She slams it shut herself.*)

TED. (*To Bonny; through the "window."*) Still want to go to the Cyclone?
BONNY. I don't know . . . (*Ted moodily gets into the "car." Elsie comes out with her book, settles* D.L. *in chair to read.*)
TED. Or do you want to just sit out here, in the middle of nowhere?
BONNY. Maybe you'd better take me back, Ted.
TED. Knew it. Home to Daddy, eh? (*They drive. Bonny looks out the window. Ted turns on the "car radio." Music comes up: a wartime song like "Praise the Lord and Pass the Ammunition." Grace comes out from* U.L., *carrying sweater and purse. She comes* D. *to comb her hair, as if in a "mirror."*)
ELSIE. Where are you going?
GRACE. Mr. McAlister very sweetly asked me to go to the movies.
ELSIE. To *Dumbo*?
GRACE. *Dumbo*? I thought it was *Now Voyager.*
ELSIE. By the way, Mrs. Blackburn called. She says the Latin situation is beyond repair.
GRACE. Oh dear. Where is he?
ELSIE. Out with the gang.
GRACE. At least it's with them.
TED. (*In "car."*) Maybe I should get someone else to ride the Cyclone.
BONNY. Maybe you should.
ELSIE. (*To Grace.*) You should write Daddy about him.
GRACE. I don't want to worry him.
ELSIE. But he's a *man*. He could help.
GRACE. Maybe . . .
ELSIE. If you don't write him, I will, Mother.
GRACE. Now this is *my* problem, Elsie, and I'll thank you to stay out of it. (*She gives her a quick kiss.*) . . . I'll write him tomorrow. I promise. (*She goes* U.L. *to stand and wait, back to audience, as if on a porch. Elsie reads "War and Peace." Music continues underneath. Anna and Charlie enter from* U.R., *as if in moonlight.*)
ANNA. When does she want you home? What's the rule?
CHARLIE. Eleven.
ANNA. All right. Then we have a choice. We can sit out here and study the stars, or we can go inside, and read selections

from the poetry of William Butler Yeats. Maybe you're an astronomer. Or a poet. Which will it be?
CHARLIE. Let me think . . .
ANNA. Now remember. It's a choice, and at your age, all choices are important. They tell you who you are. So which is it?
CHARLIE. Um . . . (*He stands thinking, Anna looking at lake. The Lights focus down on Charlie's face. The music continues.*)

END OF ACT ONE

ACT TWO

Before Curtain: Music: another old Bing Crosby recording, such as "Accentuate the Positive." Charlie Comes On hurriedly from R.

CHARLIE. This is still a play about me, when I was fourteen — (*Anna crosses Up, from* L. *to* R. *carrying a bushel basket.*)
ANNA. Come on, help me pick the peas, and then I'll show you how to put them up.
CHARLIE. (*Following her.*) I have to leave early today, Anna.
ANNA. Early? Why?
CHARLIE. We're going to a party.
ANNA. (*As they·cross.*) What party? Tell me about this party.
CHARLIE. Well, you see, my mother thinks it would be good for me if . . . (*They are Off, as Grace comes On from* U.L., *hurriedly, in a bathrobe.*)
GRACE. (*Calling toward Off* L.) Charlie! I'm in your bathroom! And I found Daddy's old razor! Now full speed ahead! (*Elsie comes on from* U.L., *also in a bathrobe.*)
ELSIE. Mother, I don't have anything to wear.
GRACE. Why not your little blue Lanz?
ELSIE. It makes me look fat, Mother!
GRACE. Now is that the dress's fault? Or is that somebody else's?
ELSIE. Oh, Mothurrr . . . (*She goes Off. Grace speaks to audience.*)
GRACE. (*To audience.*) Here's what's happening. We're all going to a party. The Ralph Wheelers are giving a big shindig for their daughter, Sylvia. It will be out at Prospect Point, and they plan to have music, and dancing, and the works, just like before the war. I'm thrilled. I'm absolutely delighted. It will get Charlie away from that woman, and Elsie away from her book, and me away from *myself*, at least for a while . . . (*Elsie comes back on from* U.L.)
ELSIE. Are you sure Charlie's invited, Mother?
GRACE. Absolutely. I called up and asked.
ELSIE. You mean, you wangled an invitation?

GRACE. I had to, Elsie.
ELSIE. But he'll be *out* of it, Mother. They all go away to school.
GRACE. That's the point, Elsie. I am thinking of the fall.
ELSIE. Oh. Right. I forgot . . . (*Ominously.*) The fall. (*She hurries Off,* U.L.)
GRACE. (*To audience.*) Which needs explaining. Guess what arrived from the Pacific last week. A great stack of letters. For all of us! Oh he's fine! He's alive, and well, and frantic to come home, though he thinks we've got a while before the Japanese surrender. (*Takes airmail letter out of the pocket of her robe.*) But this is the crucial one. This he wrote in response to my S.O.S. about Charlie. Listen: (*She opens it, reads.*) ". . . Sounds to me as if the boy should go right off to boarding school. Sounds as if he's lost his bearings. I was sent to Saint Luke's when I was fifteen, and it shaped me right up. Send him away." (*She folds the letter.*) So guess who's been on the long distance telephone. I called Saint Luke's, and I called George Graham in Philadelphia, who's on the board of trustees, and I called Sam Satterfield in Greenwich, who gives them scads of money—I alerted the whole network. And what with one thing and another, the school's going to take him. Latin or no Latin, in September. Off he goes, if we can just hold on till then! (*Calls Off.*) Charlie! (*Charlie comes out from* U.L., *in boxer shorts and socks.*)
CHARLIE. Do I have to go to the party?
GRACE. Of course you do. Now here's the razor. Have you any idea how to use it?
CHARLIE. I used to watch Dad.
GRACE. Then let's see if you can end up looking halfway presentable for the Wheelers.
CHARLIE. (*Mixing "lather" in front of "mirror."*) Who's Saliva Wheeler anyway?
GRACE. Her name is Sylvia! And she's very attractive, and if you don't dance with her at least once, I'm going to personally throttle you. (*Grace goes Off,* U.L. *Charlie begins to "shave" meticulously, facing front, as if in a mirror. Anna comes On* D.R. *with her bushel basket, settles down to shelling "peas."*)
CHARLIE. I have to go, Anna.
ANNA. Good. Go, then. You'll learn something. I used to go myself. Years ago, when my family had money. Oh sure. I was on the list. I went. I came out. I wore white. I carried flowers.

Yellow roses and Baby's breath. I danced. I was the belle of the ball. Can you imagine? Me? Anna Trumbull, the Pig Woman, dancing till dawn? . . . I didn't enjoy it, though. I saw too much. I saw into the kitchen and under the rug. I gave it up. But you go. Look them over. Then you'll know what you're up against.
CHARLIE. (*Into "mirror."*) I won't know anybody. I don't even know the Wheelers.
ANNA. (*Shelling peas.*) I do. Ralph Wheeler's father was on the way up while mine was on the way down. We'd nod to each other on Delaware Avenue, like freighters passing on the lake. Of course, their money is absolutely corrupt. Behind every great fortune is a great crime. Theirs was killing horses. When the automobile came in, old Walt Wheeler, who ran a livery stable down on Richmond Avenue, simply bought up every horse he could get his hands on. Dirt cheap. And then he systematically took them out behind the barn and cut their throats.
CHARLIE. (*"Nicking" his neck.*) Ouch!
ANNA. He sold the hides to the shoe people, the hooves to the glue people, the hair to the mattress people, and the meat, at outrageous prices, to the poor immigrants who were coming in to break their backs for Lackawanna Steel. And with his profits, he built his place out here. So when you get there, just remember: the whole shebang is built on the bones of dead horses! (*Grace comes into the "bathroom" from* U.L. *She carries a seersucker jacket, clean khakis, a striped tie, a blue Oxford-cloth button-down shirt for Charlie and a pair of loafers.*)
GRACE. I got out your suit. And here's a tie. And I ironed your shirt for you. And polished these. (*She lays them out on the glider.*) You can always tell a gentleman by his linen and his leather. (*She goes Off* L.)
CHARLIE. (*Into "mirror."*) A lot of snooty boarding school kids will be there.
ANNA. (*Shelling "peas."*) Good. Now they've decided to ship you off, you should meet your fellow prisoners. The boarding school crowd. I knew them, too. I remember the Watson boy. He was the one who ran away from Hotchkiss. He was happy at Deerfield, though. Once he was hit on the head by a hockey puck, he fell right into line . . . (*Elsie comes On from* L., *now dressed for the party. She comes* D.L., *as if she were now in Grace's bedroom, standing in front of a full-length mirror.*)

ELSIE. (*Calling Off.*) Mother, I'm borrowing your lipstick, please. (*She puts on lipstick in the "mirror." Charlie, Center, has finished shaving, and is putting on his clothes.*)
CHARLIE. And a lot of superficial girls . . .
ANNA. And then there was the Patterson girl. She was seduced by her riding master at finishing school. They never taught her how to cross her legs. (*Grace comes On from* L., *crosses* D.L. *into her "bedroom," now dressed for the party. She and Elsie straighten their seams, and put on make-up in front of the "mirror." Charlie continues to dress.*)
ELSIE. Do I have too much lipstick on, Mother?
GRACE. It never hurts to have less, dear.
ELSIE. I won't have anyone to dance with.
GRACE. You'd be surprised. All the boys are beginning to come home.
ELSIE. But I won't know any of them.
GRACE. All the better. You might find yourself dancing with Prince Andrei Bolkonski.
ELSIE. (*Looking at her.*) When did you read *War and Peace*, Mother?
GRACE. Oh heavens . . . before I was married I read a lot . . . Now powder your nose, and get your hair out of your eyes. (*Calling toward Charlie.*) Charlie, come into my room, please. I want to see how you've done.
CHARLIE. (*Dressed by now.*) So I gotta go, Anna.
ANNA. Sure. Fine. Go. While you're there, say hello to Bill McMartin. He built a chemical factory right on the lake. Whenever I see a dead fish, I think of Bill. (*Charlie crosses* D.L. *into Grace's area.*)
GRACE. Well look at you! Charlie, I think tonight I'm going to break down and let you have a glass of beer. After all, you're almost fifteen.
ANNA. You'll have to drink, of course. It makes them easier to tolerate. That's how I got hooked on the old firewater.
GRACE. (*To Charlie.*) Now come here, and let's see if we all pass inspection. (*She stands between Charlie and Elsie, as if they were all in front of a full-length mirror. She puts her arms around her children.*) There. Oh, I wish someone were here to take our picture.
ELSIE. And send it to Daddy.

GRACE. Yes. I happen to think we look very snappy. Except for your tie, Charlie.
CHARLIE. What's wrong with my tie?
GRACE. It's all over the place, my friend. Here. Let me fuss with it. (*She undoes Charlie's tie, starts tying it again.*)
CHARLIE. Ouch.
GRACE. Hold still.
CHARLIE. (*As Grace struggles with his tie.*) PLEASE, Mom.
GRACE. Just hold still.
ANNA. (*Gathering up her bushel basket.*) Yes, well, go on. Go to the party. Wear their uniform, drink their liquor, learn their dance steps. Maybe you'll like it. Maybe that's your potential, after all. (*She goes Off* R. *as Charlie suddenly pulls away from Grace.*)
CHARLIE. Lay *off*, Mom! You're *strangling* me!
GRACE. I'm just trying to get it straight.
CHARLIE. (*Ripping off the tie, throwing it down.*) I'm not wearing this tie!
GRACE. Pick that up.
CHARLIE. Make me. (*Pause.*)
ELSIE. Uh oh.
GRACE. That is your father's necktie.
CHARLIE. I don't care. (*Pause.*)
GRACE. We are late for the party.
CHARLIE. I don't want to go.
ELSIE. Oh Lord. (*Pause.*)
GRACE. Come on, then, Elsie. We'll go without him.
CHARLIE. I don't give a shit.
GRACE. (*Wheeling on him.*) I ought to wash your mouth out with soap!
CHARLIE. I don't give a flying fuck.
ELSIE. Oh my God! (*Grace hauls off and lets him have it, slapping him across the face, hard. Long pause.*)
CHARLIE. (*Grimly.*) O.K., Mom! This is IT! (*He rips off his jacket, throws it down on the ground.*) No more parties for me! (*Rips off his shirt.*) Never again! I never want to see those people! Ever! (*Rips off his pants.*) I don't want to talk to them . . . (*Throws off a shoe.*) I don't want to be with them . . . (*Throws off the other shoe, and his socks.*) I don't want to dance on the bones of dead horses! (*He is now in his undershorts.*)

GRACE. What are you talking about?
CHARLIE. I don't want to go away to school, either! I don't want to go to *any* school, ever again! I want to stay out here, all year round! With Anna! I want to live in her barn, and eat her tomatoes, and realize my potential any time I want! And you know what I want to do now? I want to go down to the lake and dive under the water and get clean, really clean, CLEAN. (*He runs Off* R. *From Offstage, his underpants fly back Onstage. Long pause.*)
GRACE. (*Quietly; to Elsie.*) Go see what he does, please. (*Elsie exits quickly. Grace goes around the stage, quickly picking up Charlie's scattered clothes. She sits down, gathering them all in her lap. She notices her husband's tie and smooths it out as best she can. Elsie comes back in.*) Well? What?
ELSIE. He ran right down the steps and into the water.
GRACE. I'm sure.
ELSIE. Stark naked. While it's still light out. And Mrs. Wilson was strolling on the beach! With her sister-in-law! Who's Catholic!
GRACE. I'm sure.
ELSIE. And I'll bet when he comes out, he heads straight for the Pig Woman, Mother. I'll bet he does.
GRACE. I imagine.
ELSIE. So what'll we do, Mother? What'll we do now?
GRACE. Do? I'll tell you what we'll do. We'll go to the party, that's what we'll do. And we'll have a perfectly spectacular time. (*She stands up.*) We'll drink too much, and eat too much, and kiss every man in sight! And when we're good and loaded, we might just sneak up on old Mrs. Stockwell, and push her into the pool! And if people ask us about Charlie, we'll say, "Who's he? We don't know any Charlie. All we know is that the night is young, and we are beautiful, and we're raring to go!" And then tomorrow morning, bright and early — no, not bright and early, but at a convenient hour — I'll tell you what else I'm going to do! I'm going to make a visit! The Shadow here is going to pay one hell of a call on the Pig Woman! Meanwhile, let's move it, sister! Let's shake a leg! We are going to live it up, if it kills us! (*Grace strides out* U.L. *Elsie stands, amazed, and then trots after her, as the light changes to early evening. Anna comes out from* U.R., *carrying a greasy kerosene lamp, a dusty bottle of wine, and two old cups. She puts*

down the lantern, pours herself some wine, and sits contemplatively. Charlie comes On from R.)
ANNA. I thought you were going to catch us our breakfast.
CHARLIE. It's getting too dark to fish.
ANNA. Nonsense. Try again.
CHARLIE. (*Hesitating.*) Why hasn't she come yet?
ANNA. She will.
CHARLIE. Maybe she won't. Maybe she's so mad at me, she's just given up.
ANNA. Oh no. She'll be here. After all, this is the perfect time for a powwow: The witching hour . . . the children's hour . . . lately what's known in town as the cocktail hour. This is when she'll come. First let her get the casserole in the oven. And wash the lettuce. And comb her hair. Then she'll be on her way.
CHARLIE. You sure know my mom.
ANNA. I know her very well. She'll park her car down by the barn. She'll sit for a moment, organizing her thoughts. Then she'll get out, and start up the path. She'll come to the fork by the old elm. Will she take the short cut? No, she will not. Little Red Riding Hood will take the long way around. She'll pass the outhouse, circle the rhubarb, notice our light, take a deep breath, and call . . .
GRACE. (*From Off* L.) ANNA!
CHARLIE. Golly, Anna. You're amazing.
ANNA. (*To Charlie.*) You see? Now *fish*! You promised. (*Charlie goes Off* D.R. *to fish.*)
GRACE. (*Off* L., *closer.*) Anna?
ANNA. (*Calling Off.*) Out here. (*Grace comes On briskly. They look at each other. Grace holds out her hand. Anna holds up her hand, in mock Indian fashion.*) How. (*A moment. Then Grace laughs.*)
GRACE. Oh, Anna. (*They shake hands.*)
ANNA. Long time, no see.
GRACE. I know it.
ANNA. Twenty years.
GRACE. Oh, not *twenty* . . .
ANNA. Twenty. Almost exactly.
GRACE. Mercy. Has it been that long? Well I mean, we've *seen* each other, haven't we? Occasionally. We've seen each other . . .
ANNA. You had talent twenty years ago.

GRACE. Don't be silly.
ANNA. You had potential.
GRACE. Oh please . . . (*Pause.*)
ANNA. Well. You're looking for the boy.
GRACE. Yes, actually.
ANNA. He's down fishing off the rocks.
GRACE. How nice. (*Pause.*) I assume he spent last night here.
ANNA. In the barn.
GRACE. He didn't even have a toothbrush.
ANNA. He didn't need one.
GRACE. Well, I imagine he needs one now. And is ready for his own bed.
ANNA. No.
GRACE. No?
ANNA. No. (*Pause.*) Want a drink?
GRACE. Oh heavens no.
ANNA. Have a taste of the local wine.
GRACE. Local? Do the Canadians make wine?
ANNA. I do.
GRACE. Anna, you were always so resourceful . . .
ANNA. The house wine, then? (*She pours a cup.*)
GRACE. Why that sounds very nice, actually.
ANNA. Here you are. (*Hands her a cup and pours another for herself.*)
GRACE. (*Sipping.*) Mmmm.
ANNA. You like it?
GRACE. Oh yes.
ANNA. You don't. But we'll pretend you do.
GRACE. Anna . . .
ANNA. (*Producing a strange, ratty, multi-colored patch of knitting from her pocket.*) Look at this.
GRACE. (*Taking it.*) What is it?
ANNA. We've been working with wool.
GRACE. Oh.
ANNA. What do you think?
GRACE. Looks a little . . . tangled, Anna.
ANNA. That's the point.
GRACE. The point?
ANNA. That's what he's trying to say.

GRACE. Look, Anna, don't you think if he had any real talent, we would have noticed it?
ANNA. No.
GRACE. Then don't you think someone at school, someone at camp might have pointed it out?
ANNA. No.
GRACE. But he's never shown the slightest interest!
ANNA. Until now.
GRACE. All right, then. Fine, Anna. Thank you. Thank you for taking him under your wing. He's had a good experience. I appreciate it. Thank you.
ANNA. You're welcome.
GRACE. But he's not the world's next Michelangelo, Anna, and he has to continue his education, and I'd appreciate it very much if you'd tell him that.
ANNA. Tell him yourself.
GRACE. I have, Anna. Of course. And I will again. But I'm afraid at this point he listens more to you.
ANNA. He won't listen to me if I tell him that. (*Grace puts down her cup.*)
GRACE. All right now, Anna, let's be frank.
ANNA. You don't like my wine.
GRACE. No I don't, Anna. And I don't like what you're doing either. And I want to know why.
ANNA. I'm a teacher, remember. He came. I'm teaching him.
GRACE. Teaching him what, for God's sake?
ANNA. What I taught you, once upon a time.
GRACE. I was a poor student, Anna.
ANNA. You were the best. You could have done anything. And you settled for a Still Life.
GRACE. Oh Anna, stop. Please.
ANNA. I never stop. It's against my religion. (*Pause.*)
GRACE. I'd like to make a deal with you, Anna.
ANNA. I don't make deals.
GRACE. You might make this one. Suppose you let him go by the middle of August.
ANNA. Suppose I don't.
GRACE. Suppose I give you a check if you do.
ANNA. A check?

GRACE. For all you've done. For Charlie.
ANNA. A check.
GRACE. (*Starting to open her purse.*) I brought along a check, Anna.
ANNA. (*Bursting into laughter.*) A check! Ohboyohboyohboy! It seems to me I've heard that song before.
GRACE. I'm serious, Anna.
ANNA. (*Laughing.*) Oh I know you are!
GRACE. I'm trying to find a solution here.
ANNA. Seems to me I remember another check twenty years ago.
GRACE. I don't know what you mean.
ANNA. I remember your own father showing up with a check.
GRACE. I didn't know that.
ANNA. Oh yes. Seems I was a bad influence on you, and he wanted to buy me off. And I told him just what I told you: I never stop.
GRACE. I swear I didn't know that, Anna.
ANNA. Oh yes. And when I refused the check, he said he'd see to it that I stopped. And he did! But not before his daughter landed on my doorstep in the middle of the night.
GRACE. I knew we'd get to this . . .
ANNA. You ran straight to me a week before your wedding!
GRACE. I had a slight case of cold feet . . .
ANNA. You wanted to change your life!
GRACE. I was a confused young girl!
ANNA. You were a courageous young woman! Before your parents yanked you out of my studio, postponed the wedding, and dragged you kicking and screaming across half the continent of Europe!
GRACE. Well I'm glad they did! I'm happily married now!
ANNA. You are, eh?
GRACE. Yes I am, Anna! And I've got two wonderful children to prove it!
ANNA. Prove it? How? By shipping them off to prison? By taking your son's natural energies and stifling them, just as your parents stifled your own?
GRACE. Oh, Anna, what are we talking about? What could I do? What could I paint? A few pale peonies in a pot. And what can Charlie do? That thing, that rag you've got? And what can

you do, Anna, really, when the chips are down? What have you ever made? When have you ever been shown? When have you ever received even the smallest signal from the outside world? Oh come on. You're a captivating teacher, and you excite the young, but this is amateur night around here, and you know it. You and Charlie have been playing in the mud, and now it's time for everyone to clean up and go home.

ANNA. Home, is it? Some home! Seems to me that while your husband has been laying down his life for that home, and while your children were fast asleep in that home, you've been sneaking down the beach to the gold star home of Bob McAlister. (*Pause.*)

GRACE. That's vicious and vindictive and cruel!

ANNA. Yes, well, look who else has been playing in the mud.

GRACE. Who told you?

ANNA. I'm the Pig Woman, remember. I'm good at rooting around. (*Pause.*)

GRACE. Does Charlie know?

ANNA. No.

GRACE. Will you tell him?

ANNA. No.

GRACE. Thank you. (*Sits on glider.*) It's over anyway. It was a small thing at a bad time and I regret it more than you know.

ANNA. All I know is that you were a woman of pride and promise, and you chose a shadow of a life when you left me!

GRACE. Oh, Anna! Please! No more! No more! (*Pause.*) It's been such a lonely summer.

ANNA. Welcome to the club.

GRACE. Did my father really stop you from teaching?

ANNA. Oh not directly. He simply told all the other fathers how dangerous I was. Somehow, my students stopped showing up.

GRACE. I'm sorry.

ANNA. And for some reason, I heard nothing more from you.

GRACE. I got married, Anna. I had babies . . .

ANNA. Oh well. Doc Holloway set me up out here. One thing about men: they put their wagons in a circle, but there's always one who's willing to sneak out after dark. (*Pointedly.*) As you also seem to have discovered, recently. (*Pause.*)

GRACE. Oh, Anna, I'm hanging on by my fingernails.

ANNA. (*Handing her her cup of wine.*) Try this. It helps.

GRACE. (*Sipping her wine.*) It's not bad, after all.
ANNA. See what you've been missing. (*She sits down beside her.*)
GRACE. I've missed *you*, Anna. I admit it. Over the years. Many times, when things have gotten me down, I've wanted to come over. Just to see you.
ANNA. I've been here.
GRACE. Lately I've been wondering what I'd be like if I'd taken the other road.
ANNA. Now's the time to find out.
GRACE. Oh God, it's a little late for that.
ANNA. Not for him.
GRACE. You mean Charlie.
ANNA. That's who I mean.
GRACE. (*Gets up, crosses* D.R.) You see, Anna, what you do? . . . I'd almost forgotten Charlie.
ANNA. I haven't . . . Let him stay.
GRACE. For how long?
ANNA. As long as he wants. (*Pause.*)
GRACE. He could decide to stay all winter.
ANNA. He could.
GRACE. Knowing Charlie . . . Knowing you . . .
ANNA. He could.
GRACE. Away from town. Away from school.
ANNA. Why not?
GRACE. He'd fall behind, Anna!
ANNA. Behind what? (*No answer.*) Hmm? Behind what?
GRACE. I want him home, Anna.
ANNA. The old story, eh?
GRACE. I want him home. (*Anna gets up.*)
ANNA. That's it, then.
GRACE. Yes.
ANNA. I'm beginning to hear drums. In Indian territory.
GRACE. I think I'd like to see him now.
ANNA. You know what he looks like.
GRACE. I'd like to talk to my own son, please.
ANNA. You've talked to him all his life.
GRACE. (*Calling out.*) Charlie!
ANNA. He's too far away.
GRACE. Then I'll get him. (*She starts Off* R.)
ANNA. See if he'll come.

GRACE. (*Stopping, turning.*) I could call the police, Anna.
ANNA. Much good they'd do.
GRACE. They'd bring him home.
ANNA. And he'd run away. (*Pause.*)
GRACE. All right then, Anna. Let him choose. But let it be a fair choice. I'll have to trust you on that. And I'll have to trust myself. Trust all we've done in bringing him up. I don't think I've lived a shadow of a life, Anna. I love my family, and I've worked hard, and I'm proud of what I've done. And if I had to choose again, I'd choose this. And I think Charlie will, too! Blood is thicker than water, after all. Or mud.
ANNA. We'll see.
GRACE. Yes. Well I'll trust that it is.
ANNA. I'll trust him.
GRACE. (*Looking at her watch.*) Mercy. Look at the time. It's getting late.
ANNA. Yes.
GRACE. I've got a casserole in the oven.
ANNA. I'm sure.
GRACE. I imagine he'd like some. It's his favorite thing.
ANNA. He's already eaten.
GRACE. That never seemed to make much difference.
ANNA. Let him fish.
GRACE. Let him choose, Anna. That's the deal. Tell him we're having Shepherd's Pie.
ANNA. Why don't you just trot out your left breast, and bribe him with that? (*Pause.*)
GRACE. (*Grimly.*) Goodnight, Anna. (*She turns and goes Off* L. *Anna takes a long slug of wine. Charlie comes On with his fishing rod, hurriedly.*)
CHARLIE. Was that her car?
ANNA. Yes.
CHARLIE. Did she go?
ANNA. Yes.
CHARLIE. Already?
ANNA. Yes.
CHARLIE. Was she sore at me?
ANNA. No.
CHARLIE. Does she want me back?
ANNA. Yes.

CHARLIE. Do you think I should . . . touch base?
ANNA. Touch base?
CHARLIE. See her. Say hello. Do you think I should?
ANNA. It's up to you. (*Pause.*)
CHARLIE. Maybe I better. (*He starts Off toward where Grace has gone.*)
ANNA. Charlie . . . (*He stops. This is tough for her.*) I've decided to let you work on my car.
CHARLIE. Hey! When?
ANNA. Any time you want.
CHARLIE. Now?
ANNA. Here. Take the light. (*Charlie takes the lantern and runs Off R. Anna takes her wine bottle and cups, and goes Off behind him. Bonny comes on from U.L. She speaks to the audience.*)
BONNY. You know where this is? This is the place out on the back road where Charlie and Ted and I used to sell lemonade in the old days. I got a secret note from Charlie, asking me to meet him here, so here I am. (*Looks around.*) I shouldn't even be here. My parents would kill me if they knew. They think he's bad news from the word go. My mother thinks he's worse than Ted, even. So I had to lie to them. I told them I was going over to Janice's to listen to the "Hit Parade." Oh God, I'm lying more and more! Is this what it means to become a woman? And why is it we women are always drawn to such dangerous men? I feel like Juliet, in Shakespeare's play of the same name. Who says this whole thing isn't secretly about me? (*She shivers.*) What a scary place this is, at night. Right around here is where Margie Matthews met that skunk. And here's where the Harveys' dachshund named Pickle was run over by the milkman. If I had any sense, I'd go over to Janice's after all. Anything, but stand around and wait for a crazy boy who's run away from his own home! But I can't let him down. Maybe the Pig Woman isn't feeding him properly. Or maybe she's keeping him in sexual bondage. Whatever that means. I've got to stay. It's by duty as a friend and neighbor. (*From Offstage, a flash of headlights, and the sound of an old car horn: A-hoo-ga.*) Oh help! What's that? Maybe it's some of those fresh Canadian boys out in the car, drinking Molson's Ale! (*She starts to hide. Charlie comes On from U.L.*)
CHARLIE. Hey. It's me. (*He looks all slicked up for a date.*)
BONNY. Charlie!

CHARLIE. (*Dangling a set of car keys.*) And look what comes with me.
BONNY. A car?
CHARLIE. A 1932 Reo. It's Anna's.
BONNY. Did you steal it?
CHARLIE. Hell no. I got it started. So she's letting me drive it.
BONNY. Without a license?
CHARLIE. Licenses are simply the way the bureaucrats keep themselves in power.
BONNY. Do you like living with her, Charlie?
CHARLIE. Oh sure.
BONNY. Is she . . . your mistress?
CHARLIE. Naw. I sleep in the barn.
BONNY. Don't you ever see your mother?
CHARLIE. Oh sure. I stop by. Now and then. To pick up my laundry.
BONNY. What does she say?
CHARLIE. Oh she begs me to come home. A couple of times she even cried a little.
BONNY. It's hard to imagine your mother crying.
CHARLIE. Well she did. Yesterday, in fact. So I had to hang around for a while. And then Anna got all itchy when I was late. That's when she said I could drive the car.
BONNY. Oh, Charlie, you've got two grown women fighting over you, tooth and nail!
CHARLIE. I know it . . . Come on. I'll take you for a spin.
BONNY. I'm not supposed to even go near you, Charlie.
CHARLIE. Come on. We'll ride the Cyclone.
BONNY. The Cyclone?
CHARLIE. Why not? We'll stop by for Ted, and make him sit in the rumble seat.
BONNY. Ted's already been on the Cyclone.
CHARLIE. No kidding? When?
BONNY. Last week. He took that girl with the big chest who serves double-dips at Brodie's.
CHARLIE. That horny bastard. O.K. We go by ourselves.
BONNY. But how will we get on? We're not sixteen.
CHARLIE. That's easy. When they ask, I'll just wave these car keys under their nose.
BONNY. But will that work?

CHARLIE. Sure. Listen, Bonny, one thing I've learned around here this summer. One thing I've learned. You're sixteen, if you feel sixteen. And if you feel sixteen, you act sixteen. And when you act sixteen, people treat you like sixteen. That's what I've learned.
BONNY. How true.
CHARLIE. So come on. Let's make our move.
BONNY. My father would kill me if he knew I was riding in a car with a boy.
CHARLIE. You're not. You're riding with a man. Now come on! Let's go! (*He goes Off* L. *She follows. The stage goes dark. Immediately, there is the sound of a telephone ringing, stridently. It is picked up in the middle of a ring. A small light comes up, as Elsie comes On from* L. *in her pajamas, rubbing her eyes.*)
ELSIE. (*Calling toward* R.) Mother? . . . Who is it, Mother? Is it about . . . Daddy? (*To audience.*) Oh I know it is. This is the way it happens. Everyone's sound asleep, and then suddenly the telephone rings, and— (*Grace comes On from* R. *in her bathrobe, dazed.*)
GRACE. That was about Charlie.
ELSIE. Charlie?
GRACE. He's had an auto accident. Bonny was with him. Nobody's dead, thank God.
ELSIE. How could he possibly . . . ?
GRACE. He was driving Anna's car, and ran right smack into a stone wall.
ELSIE. Oh Lord.
GRACE. The police said they're lucky they weren't killed. (*She leans on the back of the chair.*) Oh I give up, Elsie. I've had it. I have no idea what to do.
ELSIE. Do? Well. The first thing we do is go see him, Mother. Where is he?
GRACE. I think they said Fort Erie.
ELSIE. Fort Erie hospital? Is he there?
GRACE. I don't even know where it is.
ELSIE. Then we find it, Mother. We get dressed, and drive to Fort Erie, and ask.
GRACE. I couldn't drive. Not in a million years.
ELSIE. Mother. Come *on*! Pull yourself together! Get dressed, and while you're doing that, I'll call Doctor Burke, and ask him

where the hospital is, and he *meet* us there, and I'll even *drive*, Mother.
GRACE. (*Looking at her.*) You will?
ELSIE. Yes I will. Now go on, Mother! Hurry! Make tracks!
GRACE. Oh, thank you, Elsie. (*She hurries Off* R. *Elsie turns to the audience.*)
ELSIE. Good God! Maybe this play *is* about me, after all. (*She hurries out* L., *as the Lights come up, bright, as if on the sunroom of a hospital. Ted comes On from* R. *dressed for a visit. He carries a package, crudely wrapped in brown paper. Charlie comes On from* L., *wearing a neck brace.*)
TED. Well, well.
CHARLIE. (*Gloomily.*) Hi, Ted.
TED. (*Looking around.*) Nice sun room they have here. Nice and sunny.
CHARLIE. Yeah well.
TED. (*Handing him the package.*) I brought you some reading material.
CHARLIE. (*Taking it.*) Thanks.
TED. Open it. (*Charlie sits and opens it diffidently. It is a stack of old comic books.*) My permanent collection. Everything's there: the double issue of Hawkman, Mandrake meets the Phantom, everything . . .
CHARLIE. Thanks.
TED. That thing on your neck, you look like Prince Valiant, in armor.
CHARLIE. I'm supposed to be glad it's not broken.
TED. I just saw Bonny.
CHARLIE. Yeah?
TED. She's going home today.
CHARLIE. The nurse told me.
TED. Her old man was there, helping with her stuff.
CHARLIE. Oh God.
TED. She looks fine. They say she'll have just a tiny scar on her cheek. Like a permanent dimple.
CHARLIE. Is she sore at me?
TED. Naw.
CHARLIE. I'll bet she's sore.
TED. Naw. She said she wished she could have visited with you.
CHARLIE. I didn't feel like it. O.K.?

TED. O.K. (*Pause.*)
CHARLIE. Her old man's sore at me, isn't he?
TED. Naw.
CHARLIE. I'll bet he's gunning for me.
TED. Naw. He's gunning for the Pig Woman. He said it was her fault for giving you the car, and he's going to sue the pants off her.
CHARLIE. Oh jeez . . .
TED. I said she didn't wear any pants . . . Was I right?
CHARLIE. I wrecked her car, you know. They're selling it for junk.
TED. Next time remember to hit the brakes.
CHARLIE. I did, goddammit! They broke. Even the police said that.
TED. O.K., O.K. (*Pause.*) Want to read comics?
CHARLIE. Maybe later.
TED. There's a new one, where they bring in a Batgirl.
CHARLIE. I'll get 'em back to you, Ted.
TED. No, keep 'em. I got to give 'em up. We're moving.
CHARLIE. Moving? How come?
TED. My dad took a job in Toronto. He says after the war, Toronto is going up and Buffalo is going down.
CHARLIE. Bullshit.
TED. That's what he says. He says Canada's going to be a great nation, and we're getting in on the ground floor.
CHARLIE. Ho hum. Snore snore. Wake me when you're finished, O.K.?
TED. Yeah well I'm going to technical school and learn about electronics.
CHARLIE. Next summer tell me all about it.
TED. I won't be around next summer, Charlie. That's what I'm telling you. (*Pause.*)
CHARLIE. Oh.
TED. So when you read those comics, think of me, O.K.?
CHARLIE. O.K. I will, Ted. (*Pause. Bonny comes on from* R.)
BONNY. Hi, Charlie. (*Charlie looks away from her, sheepishly.*)
TED. He's really sick. He doesn't even feel like reading comics.
BONNY. I told my father I wouldn't leave until I could see you, Charlie. I put my foot down. (*Charlie can't answer.*)

TED. Don't you think he looks like Prince Valiant? Or maybe its Chester the Turtle?
BONNY. Ted, there's a cafeteria down below, where you can get cokes. Why don't you get us cokes? I'll pay you back, I swear.
TED. (*Looking from one to the other; saluting.*) Roger, Wilco, over and out. (*He goes Off* R.)
BONNY. Oh, Charlie! (*She sits down next to him.*)
CHARLIE. I could of killed you.
BONNY. Oh don't be silly. As the doctor said, we were young. We bounced.
CHARLIE. I'll never drive a car again.
BONNY. Now, now . . .
CHARLIE. Never! I'll never drive, I'll never go out with girls, I'll never fall in love, I'll never get married . . .
BONNY. Oh gee . . .
CHARLIE. I'm a goner. I'm a chump. I'm just a dumb juvenile jerk. I'm a creep. I'm a weird, twerpy, stupid, fairy, pipsqueak slob of a son of BITCH!
BONNY. Charlie, stop! (*She kisses him impulsively. Almost at the same time, a loud church bell starts to ring energetically somewhere. They look at each other.*) What was that?
CHARLIE. I dunno. (*He kisses her. More bells, buzzers, alarms, horns ring out, louder and louder. Ted rushes in.*)
TED. Hey! Guess what? The Japs have just surrendered! They gave UP! The war's over! Come on! There's a big party down in the cafeteria! (*He runs Off. Charlie and Bonny follow, as the sound of horns, bells, gongs, whistles, everything comes up louder and louder, and Grace comes out from* L., *now wearing a sweater. She speaks to the audience.*)
GRACE. Well, it's the day after Labor Day, and time for everyone to move in. Already, there's a north wind whipping across the tennis courts, and the lake looks gray and shivery, and we've been using two blankets at night. It's time to get back to town. (*Elsie comes out from* L.) Did you turn off the water?
ELSIE. Charlie's doing it.
GRACE. Then I'd better check. (*She goes in* L.)
ELSIE. (*To audience as she stacks the stool on the chair.*) We've got a million things to do in town, anyway. On Tuesday, Mother takes the train to San Francisco to meet Daddy, and on Thurs-

day, it's my responsibility to get Charlie on the Pullman for Saint Luke's School. And Holyoke starts the following week. So we've all got to buy clothes, and sew on name-tapes, and pack trunks, and somewhere in all the confusion, I've got to write a ten-page paper on *War and Peace*. (*She piles the furniture to one side. Grace comes out from* L.)
GRACE. Did you hide the liquor?
ELSIE. Oh no.
GRACE. Then do it, please. (*Elsie goes in* L. *Grace speaks to the audience.*) As far as Anna is concerned, nobody is suing anybody, thank God. Oh, there was a lot of talk, but nothing came of it. Seems she was already in dutch with the provincial government. Hadn't paid her taxes, hadn't put in plumbing. And of course the car wasn't registered. So the accident brought everything to a head. Bonny's father made a few telephone calls to Toronto, and they lowered the boom, that's all. The poor thing couldn't pay the huge fines, so the solution was, she sell her property and get out. (*Elsie comes out from* L., *carrying an old tarpaulin.*)
ELSIE. I think this is it, Mother. (*She and Grace cover the porch furniture.*)
GRACE. All right. Tell Charlie to check the locks on all the doors, and put the rat poison out.
ELSIE. O.K. (*She goes back in* L.)
GRACE. (*Coming* D. *speaks to the audience.*) I did what I could for her. Really. I went to see her. She wouldn't even answer the door. I left her a note, telling her how sorry I was. I even enclosed a check. For the car. But I never heard a word. Nothing. Though I notice the check was cashed almost immediately. I *did* hear, through the grapevine, that there's some cousin in Niagara Falls who's willing to take her in. Thank God for that . . . But you know something: I almost hate to see her go. (*Elsie comes out again from* L., *carrying her "War and Peace."*)
ELSIE. All set, Mother.
GRACE. (*Calling Off.*) Come on, Charlie! We're waiting! (*Elsie sits in the "car," Grace speaks to the audience.*) I do. I don't know whether this play has been about me or not, but I know I feel sad. Oh, I suppose she shouldn't be living around here any more. Confusing the minds of the young. I know all that. But still: it's the end of something, isn't it? And that's always sad. Or

do people just feel this way in the fall? (*Charlie comes out, still in his neckbrace, now wearing a sweater.*) Did you leave a key under the mat, dear, so Mrs. Marek can get in to clean in the spring?
CHARLIE. Uh huh.
GRACE. Well then, let's go.
ELSIE. I'll drive, Mother.
GRACE. Good for you.
ELSIE. And I cleared a place in back for Charlie.
CHARLIE. Why can't I sit in front?
GRACE. Please, dear. It's easier for Elsie. (*They get into the "car"; Charlie climbs into the back, Elsie starts the "car" jerkily.*)
ELSIE. Goodbye, house.
GRACE. Yes. You've given us quite a summer.
ELSIE. Just think. Next summer Daddy will be out here.
GRACE. I know . . . We'll all have to toe the mark, won't we?
ELSIE. (*As they "drive."*) Next year, I hear they're redoing the tennis court.
GRACE. Yes. We'll be playing on a hard surface.
ELSIE. And they're building a ramp. For motor boats.
GRACE. Yes . . .
CHARLIE. Turn here . . .
ELSIE. Oh no!
GRACE. Charlie . . .
CHARLIE. Turn HERE!
GRACE. Charlie, she won't see anyone. She's been very difficult.
CHARLIE. Stop the car.
ELSIE. We're behind schedule.
CHARLIE. STOP THE CAR, or I'm jumping OUT!
GRACE. Stop the car, Elsie.
ELSIE. All right, Mother. (*They stop. Charlie gets out of the "car," crosses around to* D.L.)
GRACE. Don't be too long, dear. Please.
ELSIE. (*Grabbing her book.*) Might as well start *War and Peace* all over again.
GRACE. (*Anxiously watching Charlie.*) Let's hope he's not *that* long. (*Charlie calls out from* D.L.)
CHARLIE. Anna? (*No answer.*) Anna! (*No answer.*) Come on, Anna! It's just me. (*Anna comes out from* R. *She wears an old raincoat and a hat. She looks strangely suburbanized.*) Hey, Anna. Look at you!

ANNA. Yes. Look at me. All gussied up for town. Just like one of the summer ladies.
CHARLIE. I came to apologize, Anna.
ANNA. For what? Oh you mean, for ruining my life.
CHARLIE. The brakes broke, Anna.
ANNA. So they say.
CHARLIE. Oh Anna, I'm sorry.
ANNA. Yes well, let's bury the hatchet, shall we? . . . What's that they put you in? A halter? A straightjacket?
CHARLIE. Just a neckbrace. They're taking it off next week.
ANNA. Don't be too sure.
CHARLIE. Where will you be, Anna? I'll write you a letter.
ANNA. Didn't they tell you? I'm returning to my roots. I'll be living in the Tuscarora Trailer Park. Near the old Reservation.
CHARLIE. I'll come see you, Anna. Christmas vacation. I swear.
ANNA. Nonsense. The war is over. The men are coming home. Think what they'll be bringing us: New cars. Television. Jet travel. When you've got a choice between all that, and me, which will you take?
CHARLIE. You, Anna. Any day.
ANNA. Oh sure. You bet.
ELSIE. (*Calling out, impatiently.*) Come on, Charlie!
GRACE. (*Restraining her.*) Don't, Elsie. Give him time.
ELSIE. But what's he doing?
GRACE. Saying goodbye . . .
ANNA. (*To Charlie.*) Well, the world seems to be calling you.
CHARLIE. (*Crossing to Anna.*) What about my stuff?
ANNA. Your stuff?
CHARLIE. The stuff I made.
ANNA. You want it? I was going to consign it to the rubbish heap of history.
CHARLIE. I want it.
ANNA. Wait, then. (*She goes Off* R.)
ELSIE. (*In "car."*) What if he decides to stay with her again?
GRACE. He won't. (*Anna comes out immediately from* R. *carrying an old cardboard box.*)
ANNA. Here you are. Fragments of a lost age. (*She hands him the box.*) Your *oeuvre*. Your complete works.

CHARLIE. (*Taking out an inept clay object.*) I never found my potential, did I?
ANNA. That's all right. I seem to have lost mine.
CHARLIE. (*Rummaging in the box.*) What about my tomahtoe seeds?
ANNA. (*Automatically.*) Tomaytoe seeds.
CHARLIE. You promised me some in June.
ANNA. They're in there. (*Charlie finds them in the box.*)
CHARLIE. What about you? Aren't you keeping some?
ANNA. Where would I plant them?
CHARLIE. I don't know, Anna. Anywhere. Come on. Keep plugging. And so will I.
ANNA. Oh hell. Maybe I'll drop a few over the bones of my great-grandmother, and see what comes up.
CHARLIE. That's the ticket. (*He shakes some seeds into her hand.*)
ANNA. Well. They're picking me up any minute.
CHARLIE. (*Attempting to shake hands.*) Goodbye, Anna. Thank you for a wonderful summer.
ANNA. What is this? A coming-out party? (*She gestures for him to bend down. He bends stiffly over the box. She takes his head in her hands, and kisses him on the forehead.*) There. Now scram. I want to look at the lake. (*She moves* D.R. *He watches her, then moves away, carrying the box and the seeds.*)
ELSIE. (*Seeing him, from the "car."*) At last . . . hurry, please. I have a dentist appointment in forty-five minutes. (*Charlie arrives at the "car."*)
GRACE. (*Indicating the box.*) What did she give you?
CHARLIE. Personal stuff. (*He starts to slide into the front seat.*)
ELSIE. Mother, ask him to sit in back, please.
GRACE. (*Sliding over, making room.*) That's all right, Elsie. We're all in this thing together. (*Charlie slides in, sits, holding the box in his lap. They drive. Charlie reaches over and turns on the radio. Music comes up loud: a song from 1945 such as "It's Been a Long, Long Time." Elsie reaches over and turns it off.*)
ELSIE. Can't we have some adult conversation?
CHARLIE. (*Turning it on again.*) It's a democracy, isn't it? It's a free country.
GRACE. (*Turning it down.*) Let's at least not have it quite so loud . . . (*The music continues under more softly.*)

CHARLIE. (*In "car"; to audience.*) So I tried photography in boarding school. And took up writing in college. And finally, last summer, I wrote this play.
ELSIE. (*Looking out.*) Oh look. There's the Peace Bridge.
GRACE. And the city beyond. (*They look. Anna stands, isolated in her own light, looking out at the lake. The music comes up as the lights fade on all.*)

THE END

FURNITURE LIST

Glider (Wooden.)
Armchair (Wicker.)
Bench (To serve as back seat of "car.")
(2) Stools (1 wicker, 1 wood)

PROPERTY LIST

(3) towels
Book: "War and Peace"
(2) grocery bags w/groceries
Large wash pan w/red clay
Lantern
Knitted object
Tarpaulin
Wine bottle (No label, no cork.)
(2) cups
Manila key envelope
Package of comic books (String, brown paper.)
(2) damp rags (Preset w/clay.)
Art box w/drawings, clay ashtray, etc.
Bushel basket
Airmail letter
Piece of drain pipe
Bookmark
Car keys

COSTUME PLOT

Charlie

Act I

Khaki pants
Yellow & white striped T-shirt
White tennis shoes
White socks

Act II

Same as Act I

White boxer shorts
White socks

Add: Khaki pants
　　　Blue oxford cloth shirt
　　　Belt
　　　Navy & red striped tie
　　　Light blue seersucker jacket
　　　Penny loafers

Khaki pants (from Act I)
White T-shirt
White tennis shoes (from Act I)
*White socks

*Khaki pants
Red polo shirt
*Tennis shoes
*Socks

*Khaki pants

* from previous scene

*Yellow & white T-shirt
Blue terry cloth robe
*Tennis shoes
*Socks
Metal neck brace

*Khaki pants
Yellow & white T-shirt (from Act I)
Grey cardigan sweater
Foam neck brace
*Tennis shoes

Ted

Act I

Grey rayon pleated trousers
Brown/grey/white striped polo shirt
Navy blue tennis shoes
Navy patterned socks

*Grey trousers
Raspberry/green/beige striped sport shirt
Brown canvas shoes
*Socks

Act II

*Grey trousers
Gray pin-striped short sleeve dress shirt
Green with gold embroidery tie
*Brown shoes
Brown & white plaid windbreaker
*Socks

Grace

Act I

Aqua print cotton dress
White leather wedge sandals
Slip
Seamed stockings

Add: Brown carved leather shoulder bag

Add: Blue sweater

Act II

Blue & pink paisley robe
White satin high-heeled slippers

Yellow jersey dress
Gold leather belt
White platformed high-heeled sandals
Seamed stockings
String of pearls

Aqua print dress (From Act I.)
Blue sweater (From Act I.)
*White high-heeled sandals
Shoulder bag (From Act I.)

*Robe
Bare feet

*Aqua print dress
Green sweater
White wedge sandals (From Act I.)
Seamed stockings

Elsie

Act I

Blue denim jeans
Pink oversize oxford cloth shirt
Penny loafers
Hair band

Act II

Flowered floor-length robe
Blue satin slippers
Head wrapped in blue towel

Remove towel

Blue "Lanz" dress
Seamed stockings
White high-heeled pumps
White hair ribbon
Slip

*Robe
*Slippers

Blue denim jeans (From Act I.)
Red & black plaid flannel shirt
Loafers (From Act I.)

Bonny

Act I

Pink seersucker playsuit
Pink seersucker overskirt
Red canvas wedge sandals
Red plastic hair band

Act II

Same as Act I

Anna Trumbull

Act I

Rust skirt
Blue man's shirt
Navy blue espadrilles
Denim jacket
Navy & white bandana head band
White woman's undershirt

*Rust skirt
*Blue shirt
*Espadrilles
*Bandana
*Undershirt
Multicolored pastel print overshirt

Act II

*Rust skirt
Lighter rust smock
*Undershirt
*Espadrilles

*Rust skirt
*Rust smock
*Undershirt
*Espadrilles
Rust plaid rain coat
Straw hat
Black purse

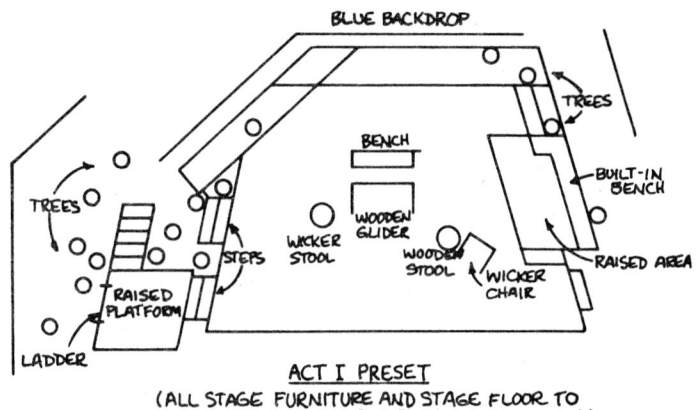

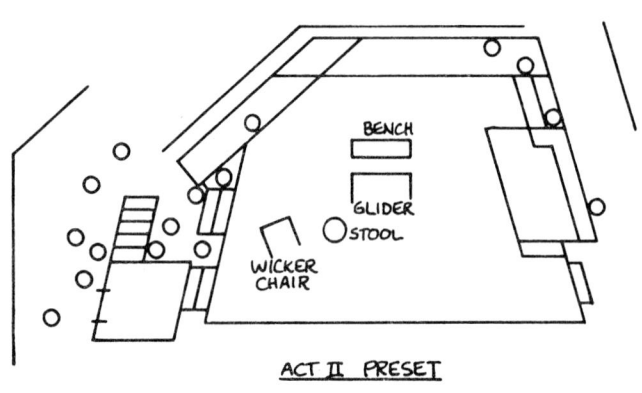

JOHN LEE BEATTY'S
SCENE DESIGN
"WHAT I DID LAST SUMMER"